A Church of Tradition

WHAT EVERY CATHOLIC SHOULD KNOW

*Explaining customs, Traditions,
Rites, and Government*

JAMES-CHARLES NOONAN

Interior Design by FormattedBooks.com

ISBN: 978-0-578-24492-6 (Paperback)

This book is dedicated to

Reverend Monsignor William A. Hodge

A priest of the finest qualities, a scholar and beloved friend and visionary

ACKNOWLEDGEMENTS

I am most grateful to those persons who through the years made a Catholic work of this size and scope possible. In particular Monsignor William A. Hodge to whom this books is dedicated. I thank also the officials and staff of the Papal Archives (formerly known as the Secret Vatican Archives), the Archives of the Papal Secretariat of State, the Archives of the Sacred College of Cardinals, the Archives of the Prefecture of the Papal Household, the Archives of the Propaganda Fide, The Papal Library, numerous nunciature officials and staff around the world, numerous priests and religious, scholars and colleagues the world-over. Special thanks to Rev. Gerald P. Carey for his expertise in liturgy and sacred music.

I offer profound thanks to my beloved late parents, James and Geraldine Noonan who still inspire me each day and to Michael, Nancy and Judy Burke without whose support my scholastic work could not be accomplished.

A

A.C.N. the accepted abbreviation for an all-but-forgotten phrase applied to the passage of time on the Gregorian Calendar meaning *Ante Christum Natum* that translates into English as 'before the birth of the Christ' and used to designate all recorded time prior to year One (or the year of Jesus' birth) or what has become known in secular terms today as the beginning of the Common Era.

A.D. the accepted abbreviation for *Anno Domino* meaning 'in the year of Our Lord' and used for two millennia to signify a particular year in the Christian era. This sequence begins with the first year, the year of Jesus' birth at Bethlehem, continuing to the present. The custom has always been to employ the proper abbreviated form, A.D.; up to the year 1000 thereafter it is assumed not to be necessary. In this Latin formula, the abbreviation precedes the citation of the actual year. In recent years, the substitution, in some quarters, of the abbreviation B.C.E., meaning 'Before the Common Era' has caused great hurt and offense throughout the Christian world. All official church decrees end with the citation of the date and year using the full Latin phrase, *Anno Domino*...

ad orientem the Latin phrase that translates to "*towards, or to, the East*" meaning the facing of the rising sun while celebrating the Mass. Sacred Scripture refers to the Second Coming of Christ which shall take place at the Eastern Gate in the city wall of Old Jerusalem and it has thus been the custom of the Church that the priest or bishop celebrating the Mass face in this direction. Between 1965 and 2008 this practice was rarely observed in the Latin Rite but during the pontificate of Benedict XVI a move to a return of honoring this ancient form of celebration has begun. This term also applies to the orientation of the church building itself. For centuries all Catholic churches were erected so that the priest at the altar would automatically face the east.

a festa the term at the Vatican applied to the ringing of the Easter bells after the singing of the Gloria welcoming forth the Resurrection of Christ and the Easter Season. The term translates to 'festively' and is applied specifically to this ringing of all the basilica's bells at the same time.

a pontificalis a gift, honor, or award directly from the hands of the Roman Pontiff, most commonly in regards to the award of academic degrees bestowed by the pope as head of all papal universities. To hold this distinction, the degree awarded must state that it has been made *'a pontificalis'*. Doctoral degrees *'a Divinitatis'* and other forms of academic distinctions awarded by the Holy See to newly named bishops and to other clerical and lay scholars are examples of awards made 'a pontificalis'. This term, exclusive to the Holy See, is the equivalent of *ad eundem* degrees long awarded by the finest universities throughout the western world.

abbé a French title for an abbot or a superior of a monastery of men. In time, this title was also assumed by all clerics in France. Eventually, all males within the French Church, including those only in minor orders and seminarians, received this title as a form of honor and distinction. When used, the title of abbé was usually followed by the cleric's Christian name rather than by the surname.

abbess the title granted by the Church to the senior superior of certain female religious communities, especially those that are known as the *Second Orders* and whose members are technically known as *nuns* rather than *religious* or *sisters*. Some of these orders include the Benedictines and the Poor Clares.

Elected for life, abbesses in the ancient monastic tradition enjoy the same powers as their male counterparts, the abbots. In certain Central European abbeys and monasteries under royal patronage, some abbesses were entitled *mitred abbesses* and were able to use the *mitre, abbatial ring, crozier*, and *pectoral cross* permitted to abbots and bishops. With the exception of the pope and cardinals who have universal privileges, even archbishops and bishops had to seek an abbess's permission to enter her foundation.

abbey an ecclesiastical foundation similar to a monastery but one typically larger in size and scope and one that is said to be fully autonomous (one not subject to other ecclesial authority other than to the pope). Certain orders routinely establish abbeys instead of monasteries such as some branches of the Benedictines, the Carthusians, and the Trappists. An abbey of men is headed by an abbot or abbot nullius (in which case the abbot likewise governs territories outside the abbey in the same way as does a bishop). An abbess governs an abbey of women religious.

abbey, territorial a combined jurisdiction of an abbey and a normal ecclesial territory which is governed in common by the abbot-bishop known as an *Abbot Nullius* with his jurisdiction being referred to properly as an *abbacy nullius.* There are but twelve of these special jurisdictions remaining and nearly all of these are located in Italy.

abbot the superior in certain religious orders of men. An abbot is elected for life and enjoys the same privileges of the office of bishop within his abbey or monastery. Abbots are considered prelates of the Church and enjoy a place of honor in the Papal Chapel. There are several types of abbots including *abbots Nullius,* those abbots also given jurisdiction over a territory and people, an *abbot primate*, an abbot in charge of an entire order, such as the Benedictines, and an *in-Commendam abbot*, one who holds the title as an honorific.

abbot, in commendam a cleric appointed by the Holy See to the abbatial office without the rights to govern the ecclesial foundation in question. This custom is rare today and is now only honorific when awarded, however, in past centuries the church actually awarded an abbatial dignity to one of her bishops in exile. These clerics were those titular prelates who had been created bishops to Sees that were once in North Africa or lands under suppression. After the fall of the church in these lands taken by the Muslims, Rome continued to keep these Sees alive by naming new bishops to them as vacancies occurred. Most titular bishops to this day receive Sees long overtaken by non-Christians so that these ancient jurisdictions may never become extinct.

Between the seventh and nineteenth centuries, the Holy See would grant the abbatial title of its hundreds of viable abbeys to one of these prelates so that each would have a source of income (benefice) befitting their station but these prelates seldom, if ever, set foot inside these houses leaving the actual governance to another. In time, this custom became a source of great scandal. Laymen, relatives of kings and princes, and unworthy clerics were named 'abbots in commendam', sometimes several abbeys were granted to one person simultaneously so that vast wealth was accumulated with no responsibility or ethical feeling attached to the foundation.

abjuration the term applied to the formal act taken to disavow a heresy that one has been found guilty of embracing.

ablegate a cleric appointed by the pope to represent him in minor diplomatic matters outside of Rome *(see also: Vicars ablegate).*

absolution the term for the remission of sin, or the penalty from it, through the grace offered by priest or bishop in the Sacrament of Reconciliation.

abstinence a sacrificial or penitential offering by the faithful, particularly involving the ingestion of the flesh of animals (i.e. meats). Although one may abstain from any product at anytime as a private penitential offering, Catholics typically abstain together as a church during the Lenten Season. Today, abstinence is only mandated for Ash Wednesday and all the Fridays in Lent and is only required by those fourteen years of age and older.

The custom of *abstinence* began in the Church in the Apostolic period in the fourth century, although Jews abstained permanently from pork products for sanitary reasons from the time of Moses. From that time until the 1960s, the Church demanded abstinence from all meat on every Friday of the year. In some parts of the world, this was extended to also include a total fast for Fridays and abstinence from meat on Sundays and Wednesdays. Until recently, the ages for abstinence was set at twenty-one years to sixty but as already noted, the span of years for those bound by the rule of abstinence today has actually been extended.

acolyte see "Orders, Minor"

Acts of the Martyrs a formal record of those Christian leaders in Italy under the pagan Roman Empire during the first three centuries of the Christian era describing the circumstances of the murders of the thousands of believers that refused to deny the faith in face of certain death. This record formed part of the notarized histories of the Roman Empire and only later took the name "Acts of the Martyrs" after the Emperor Constantine converted to the Catholic faith in the early fourth century.

Ad Limina Apostolorum translating to "*to the threshold of the tombs of the Apostles*", a visit that every residential archbishop and bishop is obliged to undertake at the invitation of the Holy See every five years. This visit is intended as both a report to the pontiff on the state of each local church and the opportunity for distant prelates to interact with the pope and the Roman Curia. During these required visitations, each bishop must also visit the tomb of St. Peter, thus the title of the visit.

Before 1965, when the number of the world's bishops increased threefold, the *Ad Limina* schedule differed by region. All Italian bishops were required to make the visit every three years, every other European bishop every four years, and the prelates of the remainder of the world every five years. After the increase in the body of bishops as a result of the reorganization of the Church after Vatican II and the growth of Catholicism in distant corners of the world, there were far too many prelates for the pope to be able to receive them all less than every five years. Pope Benedict XVI has begun to quietly move these visits further back and it is believed that in time the law shall be changed to require undertaking the Ad Limina Apostolorum only every eight years.

adoration the act of profound veneration by the faithful. As such, Catholics only *adore* the Three Persons of the Triune God and/or the presence of Jesus Christ in the Blessed Sacrament.. The faithful, however, *venerate* the Blessed Virgin and the Company of Saints.

adoration of the Blessed Sacrament the act of public worship and profound honor of the Blessed Sacrament exposed, or on public display, in churches or other places for the edification of the people. This may take place in a personal way, such as during a visit to a church or adoration chapel for a few moments of prayer and reflection, or it may take the form of a liturgical rite as in the case on the feast of the Corpus Christi or during the established *Forty Hours Devotion.* This celebration was instituted in Milan around 1592 by the Capuchin fathers and quickly spread throughout Europe due in large measure to this order's dedication to it. It was introduced in the United States by then-Bishop John Neumann of Philadelphia (now Saint John Neumann) who had a particular affinity to this devotion. Many indulgences were attached to this ritual and several popes promulgated decrees governing this liturgical custom. In 1731 Pope Clement XII promulgated rubrics that came to bear his name, the *Clementine Instruction*, which still governs how the Forty Hours Devotion to the Blessed Sacrament shall be undertaken and what indulgences are therefore attached to those that participate in it.

ad purpuratorum patrum the motu proprio decree of Paul VI, dated February 11, 1965, which mandated that any Eastern Rite Patriarch simultaneously promoted to the Sacred College of Cardinals would not, despite ancient tradition, automatically become a member of the Roman clergy (as do all cardinals) and would therefore not receive a titular church as either cardinal-deacon or cardinal-priest as is the norm. This decree also forbade the grant of one of the suburbicarian sees to the Oriental Patriarchs as cardinal-bishops, reserving for them in all cases the Patriarchal See already attained by them while at the same time granting them the title, honors, privileges and responsibilities of the cardinalate.

ad tavola pontificia which translates as 'to the pope's desk' meaning 'for the pope's eyes only.' This is sometimes also rendered as *ad tavola Petri* meaning to the desk of Peter. This is the highest form of the use of the common term 'top secret' used by the Roman Curia for items reserved only for the review of the reigning pope.

Advent a term from the Latin meaning *coming* which begins on the first Sunday of the season by that name after the conclusion of the Liturgical Year and the feast of Christ the King. It is the season that prepares for the festival of Christmas, the coming of the Christ child, and is a time for recollection, preparation, and prayerfulness. Advent includes the four Sundays leading into Christmas and although a time of spiritual preparation, it is considered by the church to be a time of great joy rather than one of a more sober nature.

ad vitam pontificis which translates in English to 'for the lifetime of the pope' and which refers to those officials that only retain their office in the church for the duration of the lifetime of the pope that created them.

advocatus ecclesiæ a common title in the Middle Ages through to the early Renaissance, similar to an 'in commendam' appointment of a cleric—translating to "an advocate of the church'— over monasteries, abbeys, and other institutes but different from the 'in commendam' appointment in that (a) their role was to defend the jurisdiction from internal or external assault and (b) they had no rights to the titles or revenues generated by those jurisdictions. Typically, this appointment went to a noble layman with a military force on which to rely in the exercise of his responsibilities to the church.

Agnus Dei (a) the threefold petition to the Lamb of God requesting mercy, pardon and peace for the Church still on Earth. The Agnus Dei was introduced into the liturgy by Pope Sergius I in the Jubilee Year AD 700 and commemorates the words of John the Baptist at the Lord's baptism in the Jordan, "Behold the Lamb of God; Behold Him who takes away the sins of the world." (b) a special sacramental made of wax upon which is impressed the image of the Lamb of God. This sacramental is always blessed by the reigning pope and no other and is often reserved as a gift from his Office. It is usually encased in a soft leather case and is worn suspended from the neck. It is known that this devotion to the Agnus Dei dates at least to the fourth century as one was found inside the tomb of the Empress Maria Augusta, who lived at that time, when her sarcophagus was unearthed in the twentieth century. After the ninth century wax from the previous year's Pascal Candle was melted down to make them and the popes began to send them throughout the world wherever the church began to flourish. This papal blessing traditionally took place on the Wednesday of Easter Week but no indulgence was attached to it.

aisle the parallel space on either side of the main nave of a church, often times divided by columns, pylons, pilasters, arches or piers.

Alexandrine Rite The formula used by the Catholic Coptic Christians in both Egypt and throughout the Coptic diaspora. After Vatican II, the rite of the Alexandrine sacred liturgy was generally suppressed with only the Divine Office of this office remaining intact. The title of this rite in use in Ethiopia is known as *Ge'ez.*

Alleluia a Hebrew word meaning "praise to God" which is sung within the Mass during most of the liturgical year, excluding Lent and days of penance. The Alleluia leads into the reading of the holy Gospels.

allocution the most formal manner of address by a pope.

All Saint's Day the day set aside by the church to honor all the faithful known to be in Heaven in the Company of Saints. As the church has but 365 days to honor canonized saints and as many more than this number are known to exist, the church set aside the first of November each year to honor all the saints. Pope Gregory III set this date to honor the tens of millions of saints in Heaven in the year AD 731. In Old English this feast became known as All Hallows (hallow meaning 'most holy') and from this term comes the modern name for the secular holiday celebrated on the thirty-first of October and known as *Halloween* (derived from 'All Hallows Eve'). The feast of All Saint's Day has been a Holy Day of Obligation for thirteen centuries.

All Soul's Day the feast set aside for all the dead of the Church, especially those not yet known to be in Paradise. The suffering souls in Purgatory had long been the concern of the church and so, in AD998, a feast was erected to turn the attention of the entire church to the need for prayers for those not yet risen to the promises of Salvation. Eventually the second of November was set aside for the celebration of this universal feast as it complements the feast of the previous day, All Saints Day, in a particular way. All Soul's Day has never been a Holy Day of Obligation but does have a special liturgical privilege attached to it; all priests may celebrate three Masses on this day for deceased loved ones.

Alpha and Omega the names of the first and last letters in the Greek alphabet that were adopted by the earliest Christians as a unified symbol or emblem to describe the eternity and perfection of the Creator. At the same time this emblem refers to God as being the first and the last, the beginning and the end, truth and perfection. Some theologians claim that this concept originated in the ancient Hebrew Scriptures in a similar emblem entitled *Aleph and Thaw,* meaning perfected Truth as a way of describing Almighty God but the adoption of the Greek alphabet, despite any similarity with the Hebrew symbol, was unique to the early Christians who could not display any visible sign of their faith in the pagan Roman Empire.

altar the table of sacrifice on which is celebrated the Mass. In ancient Greece and Rome this table was used for sacrificial acts to the pagan deities. In the early Christian period altars were portable in all places except deep within the catacombs where they were normally carved as niches in the stone.

altar cavity the official term for the stone crypt in-laid into the fixed altar in which is placed the relics of the titular saint of the place.

altar, fixed is the form of altar built into all churches prior to the liturgical reforms in the post-Vatican II era. These altars were made of stone and had a crypt inside for the placement of the relic of the titular saint of that parish, shrine or basilica. With the interior of stone, the altar became a permanent fixture of the church building, thus the term "fixed altar".

These altars were traditionally covered in marbles, mosaics, or other fine stones. After the liturgical reforms, the main altar of sacrifice inside a church was taken from the fixed position and turned to face the public. Some of these altars are fixed in that they are made of stone, contain a crypt for the saint's relic and are faced in rich stone and marbles that render it impossible to move while others in the new form were created as *portable altars.*

altar frontal typically a richly carved, portable wooden display featuring religious scenes used to focus the faithful during the sacrifice of the Mass. These are affixed to the front of the altar, visible to all present, and can be changed with the liturgical season. The most familiar altar frontal in use today is that affixed to the outdoor altar when the pope celebrates Mass in Saint Peter's Square.

altar lamp the lamp required to burn continuously in the presence of the Blessed Sacrament and more often referred to as the *sanctuary lamp* in modern usage. It came into the church from the ancient Hebrews who mandated that an 'altar lamp' filled with the finest and purest of olive oils should burn continuously to honor the presence of the Almighty within the Temple.

altar, portable before the liturgical reforms following Vatican II, a portable altar was one used in unique settings on a temporary basis, such as for an outdoor Mass where vast crowds would attend. These altars were not permitted at any other time and were dismantled after that usage. Today, a portable altar might be either this original form or may be set up on permanent bases inside the chancel of a great church as the altar of sacrifice even though a fixed altar stands within that same chancel. An example of the latter form of the portable altar would be found in the Basilica of the National Shrine of the Immaculate Conception in Washington, DC. There stands a superb example of a fixed altar underneath a grand baldachino but it has been determined that this altar is placed too far back into the chancel and is not readily accessible to the faithful. Rather than to dismantle this original altar, replacing it with a new fixed altar in the desired setting, a wooden form covered in cloth takes its place closer to the body of the church. The most famous of the portable altars, however, is the one set up in Saint Peter's Square when the pope wishes to celebrate Mass outside for larger crowds.

altarpiece a painting or architectural fixture placed behind an altar for decorative purposes. (See also *Rererdos)*

altar, privileged an altar that a pope has endowed with the grace of a plenary indulgence granted to any celebrant of the Mass upon it as well as to all those in attendance. These altars are mostly found in Europe as the custom of creating new ones passed out of disuse before major churches were constructed elsewhere throughout the Catholic world.

ambo a term from the Greek meaning mound, mountain, or hill that came into the church in the twelfth century when Pope Innocent III (1198-1216) used it to refer to the pulpit from which a deacon proclaims the Gospel. Today it is more or less interchangeable with the terms lectern or pulpit.

ambrey also known as *aumbrey,* the title of a niche in the stone wall of the sanctuary of old churches where the holy oils were stored in ornate glass cases.

Ambrosian Chant the melodies developed at Milan for use in the liturgies of the church there, known as the Ambrosian Rite in honor of Saint Ambrose who developed it. Ambrose wrote many of the melodies himself but much of the words of these chants came from the Scriptures, old and new. The Ambrosian Chant form was the first to make use of a cantor or two during the responsorial psalm who thereafter led the people in further response.

Ambrosian Rite also known as the Milanese Rite was the historic liturgical rite used throughout Lombardy in Northern Italy. It takes it name from Saint Ambrose, twefth bishop of Milan (AD 374 – 397).

ambulatory a large walkway, or series of connecting aisles around the interior perimeter of a building, especially the circular passage behind a church's chancel or sanctuary.

Amen one of the few Hebrew words that came into the church unchanged in any way. The term translates into English as the 'act of confirmation' or the 'ability to strengthen' and is used both in Sacred Scripture and in the liturgy of the church as the strongest form of affirmation of that text which precedes it.

ampullæ the term applied to vessels containing the dried blood of those believed to be saints; a form of relic. Many such vessels were found in the ancient catacombs but the most famous relic in ampullæ form is that of the blood of Saint Januarius of Naples, which miraculously liquefies each year on his feast day for one day.

anchor is an ancient symbol of safety and was such in both pagan and Jewish art and writings before the birth of Jesus. In the first century after Christ's resurrection, when the infant church suffered tremendous persecution, Christians sought out numerous inane symbols that secretly represented belief in Christ and membership in His church. It was at this time that the anchor was transformed into a Christian symbol and thereafter took on the meaning of 'hope'. It remains the main heraldic and spiritual symbol in Catholicism for the attribute of Hope and the Promise of Salvation.

Angelus a prayer ritual of ancient origin that honors the Incarnation of Our Blessed Lord. It is recited morning, noon, and evening, beginning at the toning of a bell known properly in the church as the *Angelus Bell.* It consists of a threefold repetition of the Ave Maria (Hail Mary) prayer with the insertion of several verses, responses and further prayers. Like many formula devotions of the church, it takes its title from the opening words of the ritual, which in Latin is rendered as "Angelus Dominus nuntiavit Mariæ" (the angel of the Lord declared unto Mary).

The Angelus is believed to have first appeared in the Diocese of Parma in 1318 as a special prayer for peace. At that time, the prayer was only recited in the morning. Then, during the mid-fifteenth century the prayer was also recited each Friday at noon for the same purpose. In 1456 Pope Callistus III ordered it recited each noon and later that same year extended the devotion to morning, noon, and evening on each weekday, the evening recital to take place at the ringing of the curfew bell when all outdoor society ended for the day.

Today the Angelus is recited throughout the church, in convents, monasteries, seminaries and private homes. It is also recited within the Vatican as the entire Roman Curia comes to halt each noon to recite it within the individual offices of the church's government. The most famous opportunity to participate in the recital of the Angelus prayer takes place each Sunday at noon underneath the window of the pope's private apartment as popes fro generations have come to recite the Angelus in St. Peter's Square with all present to participate.

Annuario Pontificio the annual yearbook of the Church Universal published in February of each calendar year including information on the offices and staffs of the Holy See, a listing of all the cardinals, patriarchs, archbishops and bishops of the world, the addresses of all dioceses and papal offices, and lists identifying the diplomatic personal both accredited to the Holy See by foreign governments and by the Holy See to foreign capitals. It also includes all the most vital statistics of the Church gathered during the previous year including the numbers of baptisms, ordinations, creations of new bishops, the numbers of Catholics in each region of the world, the numbers of religious men and women and other facts.

The *Annuario* is the first source of information used by the Church and is published at the Vatican by the *Editrice Vaticano.*

anthem a special hymn featuring sacred music and scriptural text, typically of a triumphal nature.

antiphon is a term adapted from the Greek meaning 'return chant' and is applied in sacred liturgies to the responses sung, chanted, or spoken by the people in response to psalms or acclamations taken from Sacred Scripture. The most familiar of these is the *Communion Antiphon* which is spoken or chanted at the time that the priest or bishop begins to distribute Holy Communion. The church created a special book, the *Antiphonary,* a name taken from the Latin *antiphonarius liber, in which all* *of the antiphons approved for use in the church have been collected according to the liturgical season and calendar.*

apologetics a form of theological science, or philosophical argument, in the defense of Christian doctrine taking its name from the Greek, *apologetikos,* meaning to defend.

Apostasy a Fide the act of a Christian formally abandoning the faith for one that does not embrace Jesus Christ as Son of God and Savior of Man such as Judaism, Islam, or Buddhism or for a state in life that denies the existing of God in any form.

apostolate the work of the Apostles and now applied to the work of anyone serving the church in a formal capacity.

apostolic churches in the Western understanding, those local churches actually founded or governed by on of the Apostles. Those recognized as such are for Saint Peter: Jerusalem, Antioch, and Rome. For Saint Thomas: ancient Guduphara (comprising modern day Afghanistan, Punjab, Pakistan and Sind in India). For Saint James the Greater, Jerusalem, and for Saint John the Beloved: Jerusalem and Ephesus. Saint Paul has the longest list of recognizable churches founded by him or at which he worked extensively including: Antioch, Iconium, and Lystra. Derbe, Troas (in Asia Minor) Ephesus, Athens, Corinth, Philippi, Thessalonica and Rome.

apostolic college the term applied to the Twelve Apostles as a body ordained and entrusted by Christ to spread the kingdom of God. Once speaks of the Apostles as a college only in theological terms, referring to their rights and powers as the first bishops of the church. When speaking in historical or individual terms, one refers to the Apostles collectively or one or more specifically. The theological understanding of the *Apostolic Succession* derives from the theological understanding of this body.

apostolic fathers those followers of the original Apostles that lived amongst them and worked along side them and who were at the same time greatly influenced by them. These men lived in the last part of the first century and/or the first half of the second century and in their writings we find some of the greatest wisdom in Christian dogma. Amongst the Apostolic Fathers of the Church are: Ignatius of Antioch, Polycarp of Smyrna, and Clement of Rome.

Apostolic Palace or to give it its proper title, the Vatican Apostolic Palace, a vast complex comprising numerous conjoined palatial buildings built over a period of eight hundred years and that together house the institution of the papacy and serve as the home of the Roman Pontiff. In historical terms, the title 'Apostolic Palace' was applied to any palace occupied by a pope on a permanent basis. As such, the Apostolic Lateran Palace, the Apostolic Palace at Avignon (informally known as the Palais des Papes), and the Apostolic Palace on the Quirinale have all held this title in the past. Castel Gandolfo, however, has never held this distinction as it has always been designated as a papal summer home and thus took the title of the Papal Villa at Castel Gandolfo (although it is much more than a mere villa). Only the Vatican Palace now holds the designation of 'Apostolic Palace' and this complex, it has been reported, contains more than ten thousand rooms, most of which are employed as museum galleries or curia offices; most notable of these being the offices of the Secretariat of State of His Holiness. The private Papal Apartment comprises a small set of rooms overlooking Saint Peter's Square and is anything other than palatial. Numerous high officials are also housed here, including a rather grand apartment reserved for the Cardinal-Secretary of State.

apostolic pardon sometimes also known (incorrectly) as the Apostolic Blessing, the final blessing given to a member of the church after receiving the Last Rites. This special blessing carries with it the plenary indulgence and its normal freedom from penalty of earthly sin. As this is normally reserved for the moment of death (*in articulo mortis*), the Apostolic Pardon is traditionally the last blessing a priest gives to the dying.

Apostolic See a formal title applied to the papal institution and until the Second Vatican Council the more popular term for the pope's jurisdiction based in Rome. Although not abolished, the church has since 1965 preferred to refer to the pope's jurisdiction as the *Holy See.* The two terms are actually interchangeable, one not taking more importance than the other, although few official documents now make use of the title of 'Apostolic See.'

apostolic succession the unbroken line of succession of the bishops of the Catholic Church from those most immediately consecrated back to the Apostolic College. The Catholic Church has claimed for centuries that this line has never been broken, and as each bishop of the church must be consecrated by another, a doctrine in effect from the outset of the Christian age, this is indeed most probable. As the church's archives reach back into history at least to the time prior to the Protestant Reformation, it can be proven that long before there were other Christian churches of note, each bishop had be so consecrated by a sitting bishop. Records subsequent to this time list each consecrator by name. The Apostolic Succession is considered to be a 'family genealogy' of sorts for new bishops, each wishing to know who came before them in their particular branch of the two millennia-old episcopal institution.

apostolic vicar a cleric appointed by the pope to represent him in minor ecclesial matters outside of Rome.

apostolic visitor a title for one of the postings within the Vatican diplomatic service used when the Holy See wishes to use a papal legate rather than an official nuncio for the short term. When such an official is appointed to a nation, region or organization, his mandate usually has a term limit attached to it as well as very specific and limited responsibilities for that duration. This title is also applied when the pope wishes to send a high ranking prelate to investigate complaints made about a sitting bishop, abbot or conventual superior. In these instances the apostolic visitor usually arrives in secrecy unannounced. Finally, the title is sometimes applied when the Holy See wishes to study the work, and the members, of a religious order in a particular region not normally under Vatican supervision.

apostolicatus the ancient Latin word for the modern understanding of 'pontificate.'

apse a semicircular extension in the wall of a church or cathedral, normally found in, or behind, the chancel. Minor apses are sometimes found in the cross aisle of large cathedrals and are sometimes used as separate chapels or as burial crypts for clerics and notables.

apse chapel one or more small shrines, or chapels, within the chancel of a great church reached typically by the ambulatory and which are created in a semi-circular or arched manner so that the altar of the shrine is fixed to the narrow point of the stone exterior wall, typically underneath a narrow stained-glass window. In cathedrals, these chapels are often used as the burial places for cardinals, archbishops, bishops and the royalty of the place, these tombs being placed in the floor between the ambulatory and the shrine's altar.

Aramaic the mother tongue, or language, of Jesus Christ and most of the people of the Holy Land in Biblical times, although scholars believe that Christ also understood ancient Greek (the language of scholars) and classical Latin (the language of the conquering Roman Empire) and Hebrew (the language of the Jewish scriptural texts). From the Afro-Asiatic family of languages more than three thousand years old, Aramaic is one of many languages in the sub-category of the Semitic tongues that also included all the Canaanite languages including Hebrew. Aramaic developed over a period of thirty centuries with various dialects differing by region so that Christ and the Apostles would have also been familiar with the Judean dialect, the Samaritan dialect, and Galilean Aramaic amongst others. In time, the Jews adopted Hebrew as their predominant native tongue and Aramaic began its decline. Today, only half a million people understand the language, which is not generally taught in schools. Most of those that still converse in Christ's own language live in remote villages in Syria, but it is also spoken as far a-field as Armenia, the Republic of Georgia, and in Azerbaijan.

arcade a series of arches traditionally found alongside a side aisle.

arch a closure in a rounded or pointed form, sometimes designed to be decorative in style that caps two columns. Common arch types in Catholic architecture are rounded, flying buttress, basket, Islamic, and segmental arches.

archconfraternities see: *confraternities*

archdean a discontinued title in the Catholic Church, a post that was once granted to prelates of noble standing with precedence over and above the post of dean of a chapter of canons.

archdeacon a title and office in the church from the fourth century to the fifteenth responsible for the administration of the work and ministry of all deacons within a given jurisdiction. The archdeacon in each place was also given the right to make visitations of all the local clergy on behalf of the local bishop whose senior confident he was. The archdeacon was simultaneously one of the senior judges of any diocese. By the late seventh century many large dioceses were divided into 'sub-deaconates' or sub-jurisdictions so as to make for easier administration. This system and the titles attached to it were abolished in the Latin Rite when the deaconate disappeared from use. In the eastern church, however, the office became more or less a ceremonial one after the ninth century. The sub-divisions created for the diaconal system became known as 'Deaneries' with each head of jurisdiction taking the name 'Dean.' The church still makes use of the local deaneries.

archdiocese a jurisdiction headed by an archbishop normally consisting of a large region or territory. An archdiocese may be titular (in name only) or residential. A residential archdiocese is a jurisdiction in the full sense of the term. A metropolitan archdiocese has several dioceses attached to it; together these form an ecclesial province. These attached dioceses are referred to as Suffrigan Sees. Some archdioceses are immediately subject to the Holy See, meaning that they do not report to anyone other than to the pope and do not have any dioceses attached to it.

archeparchy the equivalent of an archdiocese within the Eastern Rites.

archimandrite the title of a canonical superior of a monastery in the Eastern Rite churches, such as the Greek Melkites and Byzantines. It is also granted in these churches as a courtesy title to those priests of high station or office in the same way the Latin Rite nominates an important priest a monsignor. The title comes from the Greek meaning 'ruler of a monastery.'

archpriest once the title of the oldest and/or most senior priest within a jurisdiction to signal this cleric out for his wisdom and experience. He served the local bishop as his highest and most trusted collaborator and represented him in the bishop's absence. This post came into the Latin Rite from the Greek Church in the second century remaining a formal position in every See from the fourth century until the eleventh. After that time, the role of assistant, or auxiliary, bishop fully developed and the position of dean of the chapters of canons likewise grew in prestige thus leading to the gentle demise of this older office. Today, the title is rare and purely honorific. The most famous title of archpriest is vested in the rector of Saint Peter's in Rome who is properly known as the *Archpriest of the Vatican Basilica.*

armelausa long mantle, or cloak, with openings at the sleeves that was worn by all the magistrates and judges of both the Roman and Byzantine empires and which is the origins of all legal robes today. In the ancient empires they were always made of scarlet, which came into the Church for the dress of canonical judges as early as the fifth century. Original armelausa were lined and trimmed in ermine and other furs, which is still the custom for legal dress in the Roman Rota as well as in most of the high courts of Europe.

Ascension, feast of also known as Ascension Thursday, a Holy Day of Obligation commemorating the Ascension of Our Lord into Heaven. Although in many places the feast has been translated to the nearest Sunday, technically the Feast of the Ascension takes place on the fortieth day after Easter. Originally known as the *analepsis,* a Greek term meaning "to take up' the term Ascension came into the church in the fifth century.

asceticism the adherence to ancient principles in which the lower nature of mankind, that is to say the forces of nature upon individuals, was abhorred and required strict discipline to control. Those who adhered to the philosophy of *asceticism* practiced strict observance of chastity, fasting, abstinence, continuous, ritualistic prayer, and chastisement of the human body as artillery against the forces of nature that bring down man.

Ascetics, as these believers were known, found a closeness with God in this form that they did not believe was available to them otherwise. Many of the earliest forms of religious life, especially those in the second and third century, followed this philosophy. Later, several monastic orders, mendicants, and congregations adopted a symbolic form of this philosophy but they did so as a penitential gesture rather than as a way of life and in doing so, never took these principles to the extreme as was the case in the early Church.

ashes, blessed perhaps the most recognizable of the sacramentals of the church, used only on Ash Wednesday to mark the foreheads of believers as the Lenten Season opens. As the theological concept of penance and ashes were closely linked in the Old Testament, it is probable that this penitential Lenten rite entered the church in the first century from converts from Judaism. Originally, ashes were only imposed in a public act of retribution, reserved for severe sinners who had to present themselves at the church door during Lent dressed in sackcloth so that a healthy portion of ashes could be heaped upon their heads. This was originally clearly intended as a public humiliation but by the eleventh century all Christians began to participate in this ritual. Today blessed ashes are applied to the forehead of any Christian that presents himself to the church on Ash Wednesday but in papal ceremonies, the ashes are still sprinkled on the crown of the heads of those that present themselves to either the pontiff or other ministers assisting him at the *Cendres* (Ash Wednesday) service, in remembrance of the origins of this penitential custom. The ashes for the Ash Wednesday rites come from the burning of the blessed palms used the previous years on Palm Sunday and are traditionally blessed by the pastor on the Sunday leading into Ash Wednesday and again during the actual ritual on that day as well. For the imposition of blessed ashes, one of several prayer formulas currently in use is: "Remember man that thou art dust and to dust thou shall return."

Ash Wednesday is known in Italian as *mercoledi delle ceneri,* in French as *mercredi des cendres,* and in Spanish as *miécoles de ceniza.* Since the pontificate of John XXIII, the ancient rituals of the opening of the Lenten season which begin with a solemn procession of the Papal Chapel from the monastery of Sant'Anselmo on the Avventine Hill across to the Basilica of Santa Sabina where in imposition of the ashes and Mass takes place, has resumed.

asperges the liturgical ritual of the sprinkling of blessed, or holy, water at the opening of the Mass. The term asperges is a Latin one taken from the sacred texts (Psalm 50): "Thou shall sprinkle me with hyssop, and I shall be made clean, thou shall wash me and I shall be whiter than snow." The sprinkling rite reminds us of our baptism and came into general use in the church in the ninth century. Church protocol extends this custom to royals and heads of state in a unique way. When these personages arrive at a church, the bishop or priest greets them at the door with the aspergillum in order that they may partake of this rite before all others.

assessment, diocesan the title of the annual payment made by each parish to a diocese, once called the *cathedraticum*.

Assistant to the Papal Throne a special honorific granted for life to clergy and in rare instances to the laity, by the pope. Those awarded this title were automatically created papal counts as well and those clerics so honored took precedence in Rome after the Sacred College of Cardinals although at certain ceremonies they processed in closer proximity to him than did the cardinals. Before the reforms following the Second Vatican Council, all ranks of the clergy could be so honored. If they were simple priests at the time of their nomination than they were automatically raised to the office of Domestic Prelate (today known as Prelate of Honor). Today, this honor is bestowed on archbishops alone.

Precedence in this special college derives from the date of appointment not the rank within the clergy of the recipient, which is now more or less a mute point as all nominees must be archbishops. Since a reform of this honorific made by Pope John XXIII in 1960, a cleric must be either twenty-five years a bishop or both fifty years a priest and also a bishop in order to be considered eligible for this appointment.

When a pope honors a layman in the same way, they are entitled **Prince Assistants to the Papal Throne.** This honorific was routinely awarded to the heads of the princely houses of Orsini and the Colonna but it was open to other prestigious nobles as well who came to function within the Papal Court before the reforms of Paul VI in 1969 such as the Chigi, Torlonia and del Drago princes. When the honor falls to a layman, the title of papal count accompanies it, as it does the clerical honorees, although it is seldom placed into use as the recipients have been of higher rank than comital status as a norm. The pontiffs retain the right to name both participating Prince Assistants and Ad Honoram (honorary) Prince Assistants since these modernizations.

Assumption, feast of the feast set honoring the return to Heaven of the Blessed Virgin Mary, a Holy Day of Obligation in many place set on the liturgical calendar on the fifteenth day of August. This ancient commemoration is known in the Eastern Orthodox churches as the Dormition of Mary and was originally known in the West by the Latin title, *Nativitas,* which in the instance refers to Mary's return to Heaven as her rebirth.

Assyrian Rite the ancient liturgical formula for the Catholic churches in the east—particularly the Syro-Malabar, the Sryiac, and the Chaldean communities of faith. It is sometimes referred to as the Chaldean Rite or the Persian Rite.

atrium an outdoor space, oftentimes enclosed by a colonnade that is intended as a welcoming space for a great church or public building.

audience, papal a meeting granted by the pope to (a) heads of state and government; (b) prelates of the Catholic Church; (c) to Catholic laymen; and (d) to the general public seeking his apostolic blessing. Papal audiences may be either private or public in nature. Private audiences take place in the pope's apartments at the Vatican, at Castel Gandolfo, or at a residence where he may be visiting temporarily. Public audiences may take place in any manner of place where people gather in large numbers to greet the pope—the two most common of latter type being inside the Paul VI Audience Hall in Vatican City or in Saint Peter's Square. Traditionally, when in Rome, the pope receives pilgrims in open audience every Wednesday morning.

auditor the one charged to listen, or to hear, thus advisor to a high-placed official. From the Latin, *audire,* meaning to hear, a priest or prelate in the Roman Curia and diocesan chancery.

Ave Maria a Marian prayer known in English as the "Hail Mary" and which is also known historically as the "Angelical Salutation." This familiar prayer is perhaps the most well known of all the formula prayers in the Catholic Church. It is also perhaps the most beloved. Although the formula, or wording, of this prayer is grounded in Sacred Scripture, taking the opening words from Saint Gabriel's salutation to the young Virgin Mary, as well as the subsequent greeting by her cousin Elizabeth, as a composition it was not known in the early church. In fact, the Ave Maria did not come into Universal usage until the Jubilee Year 1500, although the original parts were cited in other prayers and litanies, especially in rituals found in early monasticism. The Ave Maria became universally known when the Holy Rosary devotion spread throughout the church as the Ave is the foremost formula prayer of this devotion. It is also a fundamental part of the Angelus prayer.

B.C. the accepted English language abbreviation for 'Before Christ' meaning the years in the public calendar that preceded the birth of Jesus at Bethlehem. The Latin equivalent would be 'A.C.N.'

B.C.C. See: *A.D.*

baldachino, (also baldachin) an architectural adaptation of an ornate clothe canopy once used in processions so as to protect kings, popes, nobles and prelates from the elements. These devices adapted for architecture were traditionally found in bronze or stone and were built above thrones, altars of great significance, or tombs. Their purpose was to invoke a sense of majesty and respect for the office they decorated.

balsam a resin or oil of rich aroma and texture that flows from certain species of plants either by cultivation or naturally such as the pine family and also the true balsam species found in the Arabian peninsula and elsewhere throughout the Middle East from which is made the Holy Chrism used in the sacraments of the Church by mixing the balsam resin with the purest of Virgin Olive Oils.

bandeau a white heavily starched band of linen, used by numerous orders of nuns as that part of their headdress that crossed the brow and which encircled the crown of the head tying or buttoned in the rear. This circlet, which gave height and uniqueness of design, was between one and six inches in width and sat above the *coif* that encircled the entire head. In some instances this bandeau was covered in black cloth to create a headdress unique to the order making use of it. In some orders this piece was sewed to the coif so that it all formed one single piece but in most orders, the bandeau was a separate article of conventual vesture.

banns of marriage the formal title of the publication of the names of persons to be married within the Church so that anyone with sound and valid objection may bring forth evidence in a timely fashion to halt what would otherwise be a sacramental marriage. After 1970 the names are simply published in the parish bulletin of the place where the marriage is to take place for three successive weeks prior to the date of the wedding. Before this time the pastor actually read the names at least three times during the weeks leading into the date of the ceremony. If anyone has valid objections the priest is bound to prohibit the marriage from taking place. The concept of *banns of marriage* was adapted in the Protestant churches by the incorporation of the phrase '*if anyone has any objection let him speak now or forever hold his peace*' into the rites of marriage in those churches. This phraseology is not included in the Catholic marriage because of the continuation of the publication of the names of those to be married prior to the wedding. The custom began as early as the end of the second century when all Catholic-Christians seeking to be married first had to gain the permission of the bishop of the place. The custom became law in 1215 at the Fourth Lateran Council.

baptismal water the blessed, or holy, water mingled with the Oil of Catechumens and the Holy Chrism and used strictly for the sacrament of Baptism.

baptistry also known as 'baptistery;' a place separate from the main body of a cathedral where the sacrament of baptism was celebrated. This is mainly a European phenomenon and typically in churches of the high gothic period. The most notable of these being found in Florence, Pisa, and in Rome at the Lateran Basilica. These baptistry buildings are actually quite elaborate and are larger than most ordinary church buildings.

This term also applies to the place within a cathedral or church, when distinctly separate from the rest of the body of the church, where the sacrament is celebrated. Sometimes, but erroneously, it is also applied to the baptismal font.

barb a soft white linen cloth that encircled the head of women in medieval dress and that formed a part of the headdress of nuns until modernizations of religious habits followed Vatican Council II. Also known as *barbette.* Not to be confused with the *gimp* or *gamp* that was heavily starched.

barrel vault the term applied to a curved, arch-like ceiling used in churches or private residences.

basilica (1) the term applied to a royal, or kingly, hall at the time of the Roman Empire and (2) the sacred spaces of the greatest importance within the church. There are two types of *basilica* the major basilicas, such as St. Peter's in the Vatican, the Esquiline Basilica of St. Mary Major, and the Lateran Basilica of St. John, and the minor basilicas — those churches throughout the world that have been elevated to the title of basilica by a pope due to their significant spiritual or historical importance in the life of the church.

In ancient Roman times, the basilica was typified by a large space with a wide central nave, separated by a row of columns on either side, behind which were aisles or ambulatories. The early Christian basilica, as typified by the Emperor Constantine's design, added an apse or apsidal space at the eastern end for the celebration of Mass and an external atrium at the west. Later in the Renaissance, the basilica form incorporated a narthex. By the baroque period, this style included a dome, elaborate and decorative side aisles, and an elongated nave for ceremonial processions, similar in design to St. Peter's Basilica in the Vatican.

basilica classifications the following are the current and historical formal classifications granted by the papacy for the churches erected to the rank of basilica: *Papal Major Basilica* (after 2006 the highest rank granted replacing the historic title of Patriarchal Basilica as pertaining to those found in Rome), *Archbasilica, Major Basilica, Patriarchal Minor Basilica* (not to be confused with the Patriarchal title for the Roman Major Basilicas which has been laid aside by Pope Benedict XVI); *Pontifical Minor Basilica, Immemorial Minor Basilica, Minor Basilica* and the *Conventual Minor Basilica* (occurring when a minor basilica is erected from the chapel attached to a monastery or convent) or the *Abbatial Minor Basilica..*

Current examples of each would be as follows: the Papal Major Basilica of Saint Peter in the Vatican (formerly known as a Patriarchal Basilica); the Archbasilica of Saint John Lateran; the Major Basilica of Saint Paul Outside-the-Walls; the Patriarchal Minor Basilica of Saint Francis (in the diocese of Assisi); the Pontifical Minor Basilica of Saint Anthony of Padua (located in Padua but not the cathedral there); the Immemorial Minor Basilica of Saint Cecelia in Trastevere (Rome); the Minor Basilica of Ss. Peter and Paul in Lewiston, Maine (the newest proclaimed minor basilica in the USA) and another would be the Minor Basilica of the Holy Rosary in Fatima, Portugal; the Conventual Minor Basilica of Saint Ursula and her Companions (attached to the Ursuline convent in Buenos Aires). Examples of the Abbatial Minor Basilica would be the Cathedral-Basilica of the Assumption of Mary and of S. Benedict at the territorial abbey of Montecassino, Italy and the Downside Abbey Basilica (a.k.a. the Basilica of S. Gregory the Great) in Somerset, England.

Only the most important Roman basilicas are classed as major basilicas. All others fall into one or more of the other classifications. As such, the terms pontifical, papal, immemorial, *et al* are derived from the actual type of church to be elevated and from the formula of the papal decree elevating it.

bas-relief a sculpture that has been created upon, or attached directly to, a flat wall, typically in Church architecture. It was found in both ancient Egypt and in Babylon and as a form of theological decoration came to the Holy Land with the Babylonian captivity. Early Christians also found it in Greek and Roman Empire design and so with it being found in all the cultures of the known world it was natural to introduce it into Catholic architecture. Typically, the bas-relief form of sculpture depicts extended events in the life of Christ—from birth to Crucifixion, Death and Resurrection and usually encircles the entire upper quadrant of the supporting walls.

béguinage the term used for a mainly Belgo-Dutch religious phenomenon in which houses of church woman lived in common under a shared spiritual rule but who entered the world each day working in careers (typically lace making) to help support the common life. These women were referred to as the *beguines.* In a way, they were neither nuns nor the type of religious women common today, but they could be called the forerunners for modern communities of religious women. These houses were the source of great anxiety in the 15th century where women typically either lived with family or a husband or they entered cloistered convents. It was unheard of at the time for women to live in common while at the same time going out into the community. In time, similar houses sprang up for men who were called *beghards.* These establishments eventually disbanded (for the most part); some of beguines entering one or another type of mainstream religious life or others returning to family life. Some of the béguinages were attached to churches or chapels but most were founded in normal houses in towns and cities.

belfry the upper portion of a bell tower, where the bells or carillon are found. See: *campanile.*

bells, ringing at consecration the bells that ring out at Mass, particularly during the elevations, were added to the Latin Rite Mass by Bishop Gian Matteo Giberti. Giberti lived between 1495 and 1543. He served as bishop of Verona Italy from 1524 until 1543. He was specifically appointed by Pope Clement VII to assist in the reforms of the clergy in Italy at that time. Giberti found his priests lacking in proper education and reverence for the Eucharist but not lacking holiness. To call attention to the sacredness of the mystery of the consecration of the bread and wine at Mass he ordered bells to be rung to both remind the priests and the people of the miracle taking place. The custom quickly spread throughout Italy and subsequently throughout Europe. Soon it became the norm throughout the Latin Rite.

Bells, the chimes at the Vatican bells ring out at the Vatican as they do in churches and cathedrals throughout the world for all liturgies and during historic events. The Vatican chimes are found in bell towers on either side of the top of the basilica's façade and in niches across the top of the frieze comprising eight openings in all. Most people believe that the Vatican bells are normally silent except at Easter and at the death of a pope but this is not so.

A complicated rule book has existed for centuries as to how many bells, and in what melodic form, they will ring for all the occasions in the church calendar. For instance they ring simply for daily service but employ a more complicated program for Sundays and Holy Days of Obligation.

The chimes ring in numerous melodies as well using a somber form for the death of a canon of the basilica or a cardinal of the Catholic Church, on fast days, anniversaries of the death of a pope and at times of national or international tragedy. They ring in a more festive mode on the high feasts of the church, particularly at Easter. The great bell, found within the Arch of the Bells on the left side of the façade, begins to ring when a pope dies. It's robust, but solemn, tone can be heard thirty miles distant from Rome and once it begins to spread the sad news of a pope's death, the remaining bells in the basilica join in. Within minutes, all of the bells of Rome add to this somber chorus, a rite that continues across Italy in due course. In past ages, before telegraph, radio and television the bells continued to ring out the news of a dead pope until the news had spread across all of Europe.

The Vatican chimes have been well-endowed by generous patrons through the centuries and enjoy today access to a healthy fund which assures that they will always remain in proper working order.

Benedictus also known as "the Canticle of Zachary" as these were the words that he spoke at receiving the news of the birth of his long-awaited son, John the Baptist. The Benedictus is one of the Songs of Thanksgiving of the Church. Found in its entirety in the Gospel of Luke (1: 68-79) this canticle or song of praise, which symbolizes Christian hope.

benefice, (or **ecclesiastical benefice**) an office or post within the church which carries with it financial remuneration in lieu of salaries. In the past, particularly in the Renaissance, well-placed clerics were often appointed to numerous benefices at one time, thus securing large multiple incomes for these prelates. Also known as a *prebends or prebenderies.*

Bible the written and inspired word of God, also known properly as Sacred Scripture or the Holy Bible, comprising the Hebrew and the Christian texts. The Hebrew text, comprising forty-five books, is known commonly as the Old Testament. The Christian text is known as the New Testament and comprises twenty-seven books. The Roman Catholic Bible differs from that used by the various Protestant denominations. These Protestant texts routinely exclude seven of the books found in the Catholic version of the Old Testament and parts of two books found in the New Testament and often have altered translations to promote the message of a given church or government.

The Old Testament books were written before the coming of the Christ while the New Testament was written at various points of the first century after His Ascension. The Roman Catholic Church relies on the *Vulgate,* the first and authoritative translation by Saint Jerome (AD 320-420) of the original texts of both Testaments—the Hebrew and the Chaldean originals. The Council of Trent formally authorized the Vulgate as the official biblical source of the Catholic Church because of St. Jerome's flawless scholarship. The term 'Vulgate' translates from the Latin as 'common' properly meaning 'most useful' and this translation was verbatim with from the original manuscripts with no additions or corrections whatsoever for ecclesial or political purposes.

Biblical Age the time when an individual reaches the age of seventy years, so called because of the unique importance placed on the number seventy throughout both the Old and New Testaments of Sacred Scripture.

bier not to be confused with the catafalque, a small stand for the casket during a funeral.

bishop the third and highest of the Major Orders and the office referred to as the Fullness of Holy Orders. There is no office in the church higher than bishop. The ranks of archbishop, cardinal, patriarch and pope are ecclesial and administrative ranks and possess within each the episcopal dignity. The term bishop comes from the Greek, *episkopos*, meaning the one that watches over, governs, and officiates. Originally those that held this office in Greek civil society served as municipal administrators but in time it came into church usage. In the second half of the first century the term for priest and bishop were more or less interchangeable within the church but by the second century the theological understanding of this office began to emerge. Saint Ignatius of Antioch (AD c.50-150) was the first to use it in ecclesial texts (1 Peter II:25) when he exhorted the faithful to obey the bishops.

bishopric the time-honored English language title for a diocese or see of a bishop, coming into the lexicon of the church in the late seventh century. Whereas the word diocese derives from the Latin, this title is purely English in origin and is applied to real territories such as actual dioceses as well as to the titular appointments. Until the 18th century, it was also applied to 'in-commendam' appointments as well as to abbacies held by episcopal prelates.

'Black Cardinals' the title proposed in dismay for the thirteen Roman cardinals, led by Cardinal Hyacinthe-Sigismond Gerdil, who defied the Emperor Napoleon I when he invaded Rome, seized the wealth of the Church, and imprisoned the pope. As a consequence of their open defiance, Napoleon denied them the right to appear anywhere in scarlet vesture so as to deny them the honors due the rank of cardinal. As they could only appear 'in negris' as a result, they were known collectively as the Black Cardinals.

black fast the term applied by the Church for the strictest form of fasting. Most imposed fasts, such as the twelve hour fast before receiving the Eucharist (which was later shortened to a period of one hour), or a daily fast within the period of Lent, never extended into the evening and an evening meal was always permitted as the Muslims will do at Ramadan but under the strictest fast, known as 'black' even an evening break of the fast was forbidden so that one would have to go without food for a twenty-four hour period or longer.

'Black Protonotaries' an unofficial title applied in the English language as slang to all vicars general and vicars capitular who did not hold any other prelatial title or rank and thus not entitled to purple, amaranth or scarlet vesture. Although a privilege observed only by some today (but not officially abolished as believed) these two classes of diocesan vicars, if they are not either a monsignor, canon, bishop or archbishop, may wear as their form of choir dress the black cassock, black fascia, black biretta with black tuft common to all clerics but may add to this the lace rochet and the black mantelletta.

This garb was the form of choir dress for all bishops before 1969 for funerals and at times of solemn mourning but it was also accorded to the vicars general and vicars capitular who were not prelates themselves. Because they were vested entirely in black in the form of dress common to prelates, they were known as the *Black Protonotaries* in English speaking nations and as *prelati neri* at Rome.

blasphemy a sin against one of the Three Persons of God; Father, Son and Holy Spirit by antagonistic speech against God or denial of His Divinity. In Hebrew law one would be put to death for such a sin and *blasphemers* (as the sinner is called) were severely beaten in the Middle Ages for doing so. Until the mid-twentieth century blasphemers were generally shunned by polite society but such social standards seem to have fallen out of use today.

Book of Common Prayer the Church of England's ritual first published on January 21, 1549 and promulgated for use throughout England. It is the Anglican Church's established book of prayer and ritual after years of continuing to use the Latin rituals despite the complete breach with Rome in the reign of Henry VIII. Its full title is "The Book of Common Prayer and the Administration of the Sacraments and Other Rites and Ceremonies After the Use of the Church of England." With little exception, the original edition of the Book of Common Prayer was in all ways Roman in substance and design (excepting the introduction of the vernacular).

Book of Kells also known properly as the 'Book of Columba' after the saint of that name because it is believed to have been completed at the monastery of Iona where this saint resided. It comprises highly decorative illustrations, in the Celtic motif, of the four Holy Gospels as well as excerpts from the canons of Eusebius and varies Hebraic terms. The exact age is not known for certain but it is attributed to Saint Columba who died in c. AD 597. For this reason it is sometimes referred to as the Gospels of Saint Columba. The beauty of its richly illustrated pages, some say that it is the most beautiful text ever produced, is such that legend has long proclaimed that angels completed the illustrations. Naturally, this historic text is a national treasure of Ireland—both for the state and the church there.

bow, liturgical a means of showing profound respect within the liturgy, requiring a deliberate, deep nod of the head. The *bow* evolved from the *genuflection* and came into the Church from civil, or state ceremonial whereby a male offered obeisance to royalty or state officials in this same manner. *(See also genuflection).*

bread, Communion unleavened bread that is made without yeast is the form of bread used in the Latin Rite of the Roman Catholic Church for the consecration of the Eucharist at Mass. The Latins adopted this round form in the third century after a few centuries using standard loaves for consecrated bread. By the eighth century this unleavened bread took on sacred designs with the pressing of the breads between heated irons embossed with images and monograms for Christ such as the Chi Rho, the Crucifix, and the INRI etc. Today the Altar breads come in various sizes and the grain used varies from whole wheat to refined wheat, thus the difference in the texture and color of the Sacred Host at various times.

Breviary the common term for the books of the Liturgy of the Hours or the Divine Office, the prayerful ritual mandated for all deacons, priests and bishops of the Church. Known as the Public Prayer of the Church, the Divine Office has been recited constantly and continuously throughout the twenty centuries of the church's existence. At any given hour, someone, somewhere is reciting the office of the Liturgy of the Hours, thus united the church and those in Holy Orders throughout the world.

The term Breviary comes from the Latin, *brevis,* meaning brief because when first created the liturgy of prayers to later become known as the Divine Office required several hours of every day to complete. In the year AD 1100 the Office was abbreviated, or abridged, so that clerics could perform the other functions required of them. This new ritual was entitled the *Breviarium* meaning the abridged version and thus the book comprising the entire ritual became known thereafter.

Brother, religious the title of a male religious who has not, or cannot, move on to Holy Orders. Some orders, congregations, and communities are comprised of both brothers and priests, such as the Vincentians, but other are exclusively not admitted to Holy Orders, such as the Brothers of Charity and the Brothers of the Christian Schools (Christian Brothers). The Latin title for Brother is Frater. This title is also used by professed members of the Knights of Malta but this order uses the title in an abbreviated, familiar, fashion: Fra.

bugia a candlestick with a handle used long ago in bishop's processions and for the administration of the Last Rites. The *bugia* is rarely seen today.

buildings, ecclesiastical canon law differentiates between various forms of church property. For instance, church buildings that are entitled basilicas, cathedrals, collegiate churches, public oratories, and national shrines may only be formally erected by the Holy See. A formal decree of erection is presented to the local bishop of the place and is traditionally displayed on the premises of these buildings. Monasteries and abbeys must enjoy the simultaneous endorsement of the superior of the religious order involved and the local bishop. Private chapels, such as those of religious orders, universities, or those desired in private homes, must likewise enjoy papal support. Parish churches, however, and all the properties of that particular place are only subject to the permission of the local bishop. Each diocese sets its own financial limitations on the amounts that may be expended for building projects within its own territory.

burse in addition to the term used for the bag used in the liturgy, the burse is also a financial term referring to a church endowment, either large or small, set aside by the donor for a specific purpose. Many such accounts were also left in Last Wills and Testaments for various church projects, each bequest taking the name of the project for which it was intended, such as: "A Church Roof Repair Burse in the sum of Five Thousand Dollars." Today, most donations or bequests are made in more general forms rather than being broken down into numerous smaller project names and thus this term is seldom seen today.

Cæremoniale Episcoporum the text, translating to "The Ceremonial of the Bishops," comprising the rubrics, customs, and practices for the ceremonial and liturgical life of the bishops of the Catholic Church.

Calendar, Gregorian the calendar of the current age also used by the church in the celebration of its liturgical year. First introduced by Pope Gregory XIII (1572-1585), and thus the name, because of inconsistencies in the long-established Julian Calendar (instituted by Julius Caesar and still used in the liturgical life of the Orthodox churches). The pope's edict mandated the change caused great tumult throughout the world and it was refuted outright by the Protestant nations in Northern Europe. England finally adopted it in 1752.

campanile bell towers. Italianate churches typically make use of a large single bell tower.

Candlemas The old English title for the Feast of the Presentation of the Lord, which commemorates the presentation of the Christ Child in the temple and the Judaic ritual purification of the Virgin Mary. It is was so-called because the candles to be use throughout the liturgical year were blessed at the Mass celebrated on this day, the second of February, each year. To this day, at the Vatican, either the pope or a delegated prelate celebrates the Mass at which the candles of the coming year are blessed. This Mass opens in total darkness, with all the faithful holding candles and the celebrant's torches. The lights are only turned on throughout the basilica at the moment that the pope, or his delegate, ascends the steps to venerate the altar thus beginning the Mass.

candles a sacramental of the Church of long-standing and of great import. Candles have played a vital role in the sacramental life of Christians in general and in Catholic liturgies, in particular, for twenty centuries. The rubrics require that candles used in the life of the church receive a special blessing. They should be used of pure (white) beeswax or of the lesser yellow beeswax. The use of candles in sacred ceremonies predates the establishment of Christ's church. The ancient Temple of Moses and that which followed in Jerusalem contained the seven-branch candlestick within the tabernacle. The more ancient pagans, especially the Persians and Egyptians, likewise honored their gods by the illumination of pure beeswax candles. For Christians, the light of candles represents the purity of belief, of faith and fidelity to God. Because it illuminates darkness, and thus nourishes life, eliminates fear, and encourages fearlessness, it represents God's omnipotence. It also is symbolic of Jesus Christ as "Light of the World". The pureness of the wax represents the purity of Christ in life while the whiteness of the wick represents His soul and the soul of all believers. Candles are used at the administration of all the sacraments of the church except Penance, or Reconciliation.

The *Pascal Candle* is also known as the Easter Candle. It is the large candle that stands at the chancel of every church. A new one must be obtained each year, which is blessed on the Easter Vigil on Holy Saturday by inserting five grains of blessed incense representing the five, wounds of Christ. The Pascal Candle is symbolic of Christ: The Light of the World and as such is always lit during funerals for the faithful.

Vesper Candles are those candles lit during the Liturgy of the Hours. Six are traditionally lit for solemn feasts while four are used for lesser occasions. After Vatican II, many churches make due with only two candles in the sanctuary in addition to the *Sanctuary Lamp.*

Votive Candles are those blessed candles used by the church and by believers in an intercessory capacity, used for uplifting the prayers of the faithful to Heaven. They are placed before statues, within the chancel and often times in the home. These are sometimes known as 'wish candles' or 'candles of hope'—all representing pleas for intercession in Heaven. Votive candles take their name from the Latin, *votum,* meaning vow or pledge.

Larger single candles placed within glass containers and placed before a statue or shrine, are known as *Candle Lamps.* These are also seen today in place of large votive candles and often bare images of the Blessed Virgin, the Sacred Heart or one of the saints. Any votive or Candle Lamp used by the faithful that is not blessed by the church is not a sacramental.

canon a diocesan prelate of high rank belonging to a body of priests known as a *Chapter,* or college. A priest who serves the bishop of the place as one of his senior advisors (a group of priests known in the United States as *diocesan consulters*) and who, along with the other canons, gathers to elect the bishop's replacement or to nominate a list from which a new bishop will be selected and who on a daily basis gather to sing the Divine Office in common. This post arose in the church in the third century. Originally the canons followed a strict rule of life and were more or less monastic, but each of those groups of monastic canons that survive to today (such as the Norbertines or the Lateran Canons) are now considered to be religious orders. The title of 'canon' hereafter refers to those prelates with special privileges and rank within the diocese.

Canons may be either attached to the diocesan cathedral or may be attached to a special church of great significance, known as a *Collegial Church.* Canons are permanently assigned to these churches and may not be transferred after their appointment unless promoted to higher office, such as to the dignity of bishop or cardinal. A reigning pope may only erect a new chapter of canons and therefore it is the pope who can only name new canons, however, as this would prove problematic, he traditionally delegates this role to either the local bishop or the dean of the chapter.

There are also *titular canons*, a purely honorific title granted to ecclesiastical friends of a diocese or of a local bishop. The award of these honorary canonries carries the right to dress in the colorful garb of that particular *Chapter of Canons* and to be addressed by the title *Canon* in place of the traditional title of *Father,* but it does not carry with it any of the important responsibilities or privileges associated with those prelates who actually serve a bishop in his place.

Canon of the Mass it is the most solemn and most holy part of the Mass as it is at this place in the liturgy that the Transubstantiation takes place. In the Latin it is properly known as the *Canon Missae.* The word 'canon" translates from the Greek to "rule" or "law" and for this reason is applied to the unimpeachable formula of consecration of the Bread and Wine into the Body and Blood of Jesus Christ. It is also for this reason applied to the code of law of the Church, which bears its name.

canoness a female religious, typically of the monastic or mendicant period, who live a life of communal prayer under the rule of Saint Augustine. For all intense and purpose they are similar to Benedictine nuns or Dominicans but take the name of canoness rather than nun or sister. There were also women who assisted at the altar in the same way altar servers of both sexes do today; these women were generally referred to as canonesses but they did not live under any formal rule of life.

Canons, Apostolic a collection of constitutions of ancient origin, the earliest dating to the Council of Antioch in AD 341, which outline the duties, responsibilities and privileges of the Office of Bishop and thus forming one of the foundations of the modern understanding of the hierarchy in the Catholic church.

canons, vesture of those prelates that have been named to one or more chapters of canons, either to a diocesan chapter house or to one of the dozens of collegiate churches (particularly in Europe and South America) are entitled to a very unique form of prelatial dress. The costume of canons varies with each chapter and those named as titular, supranumerary or honorary canons enjoy the full privileges of dress of that chapter. Although the costumes vary, canons most commonly don either a mozzetta of black, purple or red silk or a mantelletta of those colors. In rare cases, such as the canons of Seville and Monaco (the latter no longer uses this vesture) and other grand cathedrals, the canons don a raw silk abbreviated form of the cappa magna with overlaid mozzetta. In winter season, many of these chapters added a mozzetta of white miniver or ermine. Some canonries added a white ruff to the collar of their costume while others, like Krakow, don a black mantelletta but pipe it throughout in purple. The actual form of vesture depends upon the original papal decree erecting the chapter many centuries ago and tends to follow national or regional styles of ecclesial dress of that time.

Canons are also permitted the use of the rochet with red sleeves as well as the pectoral cross which should always be suspended from a black and gold intertwined cord in the same fashion as the pectoral cross cord for bishops and cardinals. They may also wear the black zucchetto, which is piped in purple or red (depending upon the vesture color of the chapter) as well as the black biretta with a tuft of the appropriate color. It should be noted that some canonries made use of other colors, such as sky blue at Notre Name de Paris and green for the canons associated with the Collegiate Church of the Order of Ss. Maurice and Lazarus of the Royal House of Savoy. All of the canons of the papal basilicas in Rome, since Vatican Council II, have been simultaneously granted the title of Protonotary Apostolic Supernumerary and thus don the vesture of this office of the Holy See's prelature rather than the canonical dress once associated with those various basilicas.

Notes: a priest may be named an honorary, titular, or supranumerary canon of several chapters or collegiate churches simultaneously in his lifetime but may only be named a residential canon to one place in a lifetime. As such, he may possess the vesture of each appointment but may only wear that which is proper to the place he is attending at any given time. Canons do not outrank the papal offices associated with the title of monsignor, although most canons have the right to assume the style of monsignor as a courtesy. Canons that have also been named monsignors by the Holy See do not outrank their brother canons because of this. Precedence within a canonry depends upon seniority and the rules governing each chapter house.

canons, form of address in the English language a canon is addressed simply as "The Very Reverend John Canon Doe" but in other traditions the title may precede or follow the name such as " Illustrisimo e Reverendo Giovanni Battista Mancini, Canonico di San Stefano." Almost always, and as a mere courtesy, each is addressed in conversation as "Monsignor" or less formally as "Canon Doe" but the use of the familiar "Monsignor" should not indicate further honor as a papal prelate that would also carry this title.

canon law the law of the Catholic Church comprising a series of codes applied to the theological, administrative, sacramental and spiritual aspects of both the Church Universal and the Holy See. *Canon law* was first codified in 1917. This law remained in effect until updated by order of Pope John Paul II in 1983.

canons, liturgical those segments of the Sacred Liturgy known as the 'Canons of the Mass' that pertain to the consecration of the Blessed Sacrament and reenactment of the miracle of the Last Supper.

canopy a covering of rich clothe that was carried above the monstrance bearing the Eucharist during processions such as on the feast of Corpus Christi (known also as Corpus Domine). When made of marbles, metals or stone this canopy traditionally takes the Italian architectural title of *baldachino.*

canticle those poetic songs of praise most resembling the psalms. Sixteen of the traditional canticles are found in Old Testament scripture while three come to us from the New Testament. All of these are found in the Divine Office (Liturgy of the Hours) and many of these came into that liturgy as early as AD 800. Pope Saint Pius X added the remainder in his reforms at the turn of the twentieth century. There are also three non-scriptural canticles in use. Giving them their Latin titles, these are the *Gloria in Excelsis,* the *Te Deum,* and the *Trisagion* (Holy God, holy immortal God, holy and mighty have mercy upon us), which comes to us from the Greek liturgical traditions of the fifth century.

Canticle of Simeon also known properly as the "Nunc Dimittis" from the first words of the song in Latin and found in the Gospel of Luke (2:29-32). This canticle is most famous for the words : "now thou has dismissed thy servant, O Lord" in reference to the promises made to Simeon that he would see the Redeemer of the world before his death. The Nunc Dimittis is one of three formulas foremost in song used in the Liturgy of the Hours.

Canticles, Evangelical the three main canticles (songs of praise and thanksgiving) found in the Divine Office (Liturgy of the Hours) so called because these three, out of the more than ten traditionally recited, are pre-eminent in terms of their scriptural significance. The three songs are in proper sequence: the Magnificat (the Canticle of Mary), the Benedictus (the Canticle of Zachary) and the Nunc Dimittis (the Canticle of Simeon).

cantor the person formally charged with leading the singing, and in guiding a choir, in the liturgies of the Catholic Church. The cantor must be well versed in chant, in congregational singing, and in chorale so as to properly enrich the sacredness of the Mass and other liturgies of the church. The original title for this office was *precentor* from which in English we now have the word 'presenter'.

Capita Ordinum the title used by the church to collectively define the most senior cardinal in each of the three orders of cardinals within the Sacred College: Cardinal-Bishops, Cardinal-Priests, and Cardinal-Deacons. Together these three prelates exercise ceremonial and canonical offices during the period of *sede vacante* and during the *conclave.*

cappa negra the black floor length woolen cape with hood common in winter season in ancient Rome and adopted early on for use in the church by all ranks of the clergy. By the fifth century, the black cape was the standard winter outer garb for all clerics and for nuns. Saint Augustine of Hippo (d. AD 430) is commonly depicted wearing it. The Augustinians, Benedictines and other later orders adopted it for internal church use as well. In time, the cape was made of better cloth for use as the mantle used during the Divine Office in unheated monasteries and thus took the name *Cappa Choralis.* This choir cape was adopted by the Order of Preachers (Dominicans) in the thirteenth century and is now most identified with them as this black cape over the white Dominican habit became quiet recognizable and is still in use. See also *Cape, Choir.*

cappella maggiore the term given at the Vatican to the larger more senior chapel in the pope's usage within the Apostolic Palace of the Vatican. Today this title is held by the Sistine Chapel although the pope seldom celebrates Mass there. Although the title is an unofficial one, as the titular or patron's name is how each chapel is still known, for administrative purposes within the Vatican the phrase applies translating to the 'greater chapel.'

card, Mass the ornate spiritual bouquet presented to the sick, or to the family of the dead, pledging the celebration of a Mass or series of Masses for a specific intention. It is the custom in the United States for such spiritual bouquets to be presented to Catholic families at the funeral of a loved one.

cardinal, crown a member of the Sacred College of Cardinals who held the special trust of a Catholic king or emperor and who might be expected to impose the papal veto during a conclave. A crown-cardinal was considered a servant of the crown as much as a senator of the church. This post was abolished during the pontificate of Pius X.

cardinal-king a title held by only one person in the history of the Catholic Church, Henry Stuart, the Cardinal-Duke of York (11 March 1725 – 13 July 1807), heir to the Stuart throne of Scotland and pretender to the British throne including the realms of England, Scotland, Ireland and the principality of Wales. When the last pretender to the Stuart line, Charles III, known more commonly as the *Young Pretender* or *Bonnie Prince Charlie,* died in 1788 his claim to the throne passed to his sole surviving brother who was living in Rome as a cardinal of the church. With his brother's death, the Cardinal-Duke of York became known as the Cardinal-King under the name of Henry IX, but the papacy never acknowledged this assumed title of pretense although at death he was accorded burial inside Saint Peter's Basilica, an honor reserved for popes, saints and on rare occasions, Catholic kings in exile.

cardinals, palatine the cardinals prior to the twentieth century that were attached to the papacy with no obligations or responsibilities outside of Rome. These prelates were typically close relations to a reigning or recently deceased pope and often times involved themselves in intrigue and conspiracy that plagued the church for centuries. The term 'palatine' refers to the papal 'palace' (in this instance the Lateran Palace where these cardinals typically resided).

cardinal protector a member of the Sacred College of Cardinals whom the pope has appointed, in addition to the other responsibilities entrusted to him, to serve as overseer for the Holy See or to serve as a liaison between the papacy and a given institution. Cardinal-protectors were quite common and almost every religious order once had one attached to its own curia but today this position is rarely granted. The most famous of the current cardinal-protector incumbents is Pio Cardinal Laghi who serves as the Cardinal-Protector of the Sovereign Military Order of Saint John of Jerusalem, of Rhoades and of Malta. In this particular historic role, the cardinal protector is more a liaison between the government of the Holy See and that of the Knights of Malta than it is the role of overseer.

cartes de visite the diplomatic term, from the French, for visiting or social cards used to present ones compliments without staying to visit, more or less a European and/or diplomatic practice today.

castrum doloris the Latin term for the device that we have come to know more commonly as the *catafalque*. Whereas 'catafalque' translates to 'half coffin' the meaning for the *castrum doloris* is quite different. The best translation from the Latin would be "mound of sorrow." *Castrum* (fort, castle or mound) gives its shape to the wooden structure supporting the deceased and the word *doloris* translates to pain and sorrow. Together, this term is symbolic of the sorrow found by the side of the beloved deceased. Castrum doloris is rarely found in the vernacular associated with funeral liturgies today, although the Danish Court used it at the time of the death of the late Queen Mother Ingrid of Denmark in 2000.

cassock Also known as the *soutaine.* The garb proper to secular priests and the hierarchy, made of black wool for everyday use and silk for ceremonies. It takes a tubular form and is closed by thirty-three buttons in the front, each representing one of the years of Christ's earthly life. Black is the normal color for priests, black trimmed in amaranth red for the monsignors and bishops while black with scarlet trim is reserved for the cardinals.

For ceremonies, the *soutaine* takes the name *choir cassock* for the hierarchy and is made either entirely of violet silk for bishops or scarlet for the cardinals. A *cassock* with a small open shoulder cape is known as the *simar* and is always made of black silk (with the appropriate color trim depending upon the rank of the wearer) with the exception of that worn by the pope, which is always white.

casula the Roman version of the Greek *paenula* said to be a forerunner of the Gothic-style chasuble.

catafalque the wooden platform in the shape of a coffin on which is laid the body or casket of the pope, cardinals, bishops, and heads of state and royalty during funeral rites or *obsequies.* Catafalque comes from the Greek, meaning "half coffin." Originally, this device was used to display the deceased before the body was removed in a shroud. In recent times, but before 1965, a covered catafalque was also used during the funeral rites for those of any station whose remains were not recovered, as in the case of drowning at sea, fire, or war, in place of a body but this purpose was discontinued after 1969. Today the presence of a catafalque is more a matter of state protocol rather then it is a liturgical usage.

catechumen a person who is being instructed in the Catholic faith but who has not as yet been baptized or formally received into the church.

cathedra or "chair," meaning the seat of power and authority of a pope, bishop or abbot. When popes speak *ex cathedra* they are speaking with the full weight and teaching authority of the Magisterium of the church and which teaching is binding on all the faithful.

cathedral the seat of the bishop of a diocese; the first church of an ecclesiastical territory. There can be only one cathedral, or bishop's church, per diocese although it is possible for a bishop to nominate a *co-cathedral,* when a great distance from the see city permits the designation of a second church to also serve as a cathedral, and a *pro-cathedral,* a church nearby the cathedral, which can be used when a larger church would be required for ceremonies too grand for the designated cathedral of a diocese. The cathedral of Rome is not St. Peter's in the Vatican but rather the Basilica of St. John Lateran.

cathedral, abbatial the title of a cathedral-church that is simultaneously the main chapel of a territorial abbey, or abbey nullius. An example of this rare title would be the chapel of the Abbey Nullius of Saint Maurice d'Agaune in Switzerland, which serves as the cathedral of the canonical jurisdiction attached to the abbey.

cathedral (royal) the title given by Catholic kings and emperors to the cathedral of their capital city so designated because this church also served the monarchy as the site of great state (royal) ceremonial such as coronations and the burial of sovereigns/monarchs of the place. An example of such a designation, which the church continues to uphold, would be the Cathédrale-Royale de Saint-Denis in Paris.

cathedraticum the ancient title for the sum of money paid each year by the clergy (now from parish funds) for the upkeep of the bishop (now for the running of the diocese) and in some Catholic nations from the state as well. This custom dates to the third century and is more a tax for governing the church than it is a salary for members of the hierarchy.

Catholic the title of the Church founded by Saint Peter at Rome in the first century and the only Christian Church in existence for several hundreds of years after Christ. The word Catholic comes from the Greek *katholikos meaning 'of the whole or universal.' The title first appeared in writing in the year AD 110 in a letter by Saint* Ignatius of Antioch to the people of Smyrna although it was this title that was generally used by the early church at Rome during Saint Peter's lifetime as the Greek was more precise in meaning than the Latin at that time. The title **Catholic Church**

(katholike ekklesia) replaced the term Christian Church by the end of the first century and did not reappear until after the Protestant Reformation took hold with numerous protesting churches being formed under Christian dogma of varying degrees.

Catholic-Christians a modern term now most commonly found in English speaking countries used to identify members of the Catholic Church as Christian believers. Whereas the term 'Catholic' identifies the faithful as members of a specific Church (i.e. Roman Catholic Church), the term 'Christian' identifies one as a believer in the tenants of Jesus Christ rather than as a member of a specific formal Church body.

To be a *Catholic-Christian* simply means that a particular follower of Jesus Christ (i.e. a Christian) is also a member of the oldest branch of the Christian family tree—the Roman Catholic Church. This term came into being after a prejudicial movement in the 1950s-1960s in the southern United States set out to disavow Roman Catholicism as a Christian Church.

Catholicos the title of the senior ranking prelate or hierarch of some churches within the Orthodox Communion such as in the Orthodox Church of Georgia and in the Armenian Church. The title of the seat of government of such officials is called the *catholicosate* while the plural for such officials is *catholicoi.*

caudæ the correct title for the *infulæ,* or flaps, that hung from the back of the papal crown.

Celtic Rite is the ancient liturgical formula used by the church in Ireland, Wales, the Island of Man, Brittany, and Scotland and which was carried throughout continental Europe in monasteries and abbeys founded or staffed by Irish monks.

chalice the sacred vessel reserved for priests and bishops in the celebration of the Liturgy of the Eucharist. The name derives from the Latin, *calix,* which translates to 'cup'. The chalice originated in clay form as actually used by Christ and His disciples at the Last Supper. It is intended as the receptacle of the Precious Blood during the celebration of the Mass. During the first centuries of the Christian era the form remained more or less hardened clay due to the poverty of the early Christians and because of the secrecy in which these persecuted believers had to exist. After the Emperor Constantine converted the Roman Empire to Christianity in the middle of the fourth century, he likewise endowed the Church with great riches and the chalice began to take on the form that it remains today. Many forms of chalice exist today, mimicking the styles of architecture through the ages; the most elegant being the Gothic style. Although many modern adaptations have developed after 1965, the rubrics still demand that the interior of the cup be heavily gold-plated if not entirely made of gold. The chalice may be of gold, silver or gilt, and even other materials are now permitted but the receptacle for the Precious Blood must be worked in gold.

Chamberlain, lay See the chapter: *Papal Honors—Laity*

chancel the place within the church where the altar resides and where the celebration of the Mass takes place. The term derives from the Latin, *cancellus,* meaning 'lattice' for in ancient church architecture this area was most often partially hidden by fanciful woodwork in the form of latticework. In modern parlance this area of the church building is more commonly referred to as the *sanctuary.* In modern architecture, specifically those churches built in the round; the term chancel may not apply as in this style no such place exists. In the old rites of the Mass, it was the place where the deacons would stand when they were not assisting at the altar.

chancellor an officer of the diocesan administration of the highest degree. The chancellor can be a cleric, religious or layman but must possess great learning and ecclesial ability. Much of the business of the diocese is coordinated through the office of the chancellor and thus he or she is one of the closest collaborators of the diocesan bishop. Before Vatican Council II, a priest, monsignor or auxiliary bishop always held this post. The title comes to us from the term "chancel" as this prelate originally assumed his powers at the altar in this place.

chancery the title for the legal offices of a diocese or archdiocese.

chant see: *Gregorian Chant*

chaplain the cleric holding the post of spiritual caregiver to military personnel, to students, and/or to those in medical facilities and like institutions. Technically this term means 'the one who has been charged with the governance of a chapel' but the term alternately applies to those that minister to persons not a part of a normal canonical parish family.

Chapel, Papal the title of the formal body of clerics and laymen appointed to assist the pope at the Divine Office and during the most solemn of ceremonies held at the Vatican or elsewhere. The term 'Chapel' does not refer to a sacred place in this instance, rather it refers to the group attending the pontiff. All cardinals, patriarchs, major archbishops, archbishops and bishops appointed additionally as 'assistants to the papal throne' and the College of Protonotaries Apostolic form the core of this group. These are thereafter joined by the Vice Camerlengo, the papal theologian, and numerous lay and clerical officials within the Roman Curia. In all, some fifty distinct groups of officials are included in the roster of those considered an official part of the pontiff's assistants at sacred liturgies and grand solemn ceremonies.

chapels, papal there are numerous chapels within the Vatican and other papal residences for use of the pope and his entourage. The most private of these is the private chapel within the pope's apartment which was originally decorated by Paul VI in the austere Roman modern style. There are no windows in the chapel but the ceiling and walls are lined with modern design stained glass lit from behind. Particularly impressive is the ceiling stained glass which depicts Christ's Resurrection. A larger chapel is kept at the ready for the pope on the next floor known as the Misericordia Chapel. This chapel overlooks St. Peter's Square below and has been recently redecorated in an elaborate byzantine style. The Sistine and Pauline Chapel conclude the list of the pope's private chapels at the Vatican, the Sistine restored in the 1990s and the Pauline Chapel adjacent to it renovated under Pope Benedict XVI and re-dedicated in August 2009. The Sistine Chapel bears the secondary title of *cappella maggiore.*

It is the site of the papal conclaves, the annual papal ceremony of baptizing infants from Rome and elsewhere, and some episcopal consecrations. The Pauline is now restricted to the exclusive use by the pope as commanded by Benedict XVI who wishes to use it for exposition of the Blessed Sacrament. Each of the last two of these private chapels is richly decorated by the great masters of the Renaissance. There is a modern chapel for the pope at Castel Gandolfo as well. It has been said that the basilica of Saint Peter in the Vatican, not actually a church or cathedral in canonical terms, serves as the ultimate of the papal chapels but this would only be so when not considering this group in terms of privately used places of worship for Saint Peter's can in no way be considered a private place of worship.

chapter house the term applied to the place where the canons of a cathedral reside in common. Also known as a *canonry* or a *collegiate assembly.*

chatelain the English term for the male owner or manager of a large manor house. The female equivalent being *chatelaine.* In the male usage, this title is often found in the church when referring to those prelates in charge of the various papal palaces (Vatican, Lateran, and Castel Gandolfo).

chemise a long white 'nightshirt-like' garment worn my many orders of nuns and religious women under the traditional habit.

chiavine the Italian term for the Vatican emblem consisting of the papal tiara and the crossed keys, primarily used by the Roman Curia.

chimere a very ancient garment worn by prelates from the eleventh century. In the Renaissance, this garb was shortened in the Catholic Church and became the *mantelletta*, or little mantle. However these changes did not occur in England where the Anglican Church continued to make use of many traditional items of Roman vesture and vestments. Today, the chimere is worn my bishops and canons in the Church of England. It can be black or may be made of color, is full length, and has slits for the arms to extend through. It is opened at the front but may or may not be fastened at the neck. An alb or rochet is always worn beneath it as this has become a form of vestment with the Anglican Church. It did not begin as such, however, as the word 'chimere' is actually a bastardization of the word *zimmara* which has come to be known as an elaborate cassock used by prelates but in the Middle Ages was actually worn open as a cloak for outdoor use.

choir the place where canons gather to recite the Liturgy of the Hours, known also as the Divine Liturgy. Also the place within a large church or cathedral reserved for quiet prayer or devotions, such as a chapel. Choirs were sometimes used as the place for the crypts for canons and bishops, as well. Known also as a *cantoria.*

choir cape sometimes also known by its Italian name, *cappa.* The long oftentimes hooded mantle worn during the sacred liturgy and at other solemn times by monks, mendicants, nuns and religious women as proscribed by the particular 'Rule of Life' of each community.

The *choir cape* has taken on many shapes and colors, sometimes seen as full while in some orders it is made to appear conical in shape. The Dominican Fathers, for instance have used a full shaped black woolen cape over their white habits in church for eight hundred years while the Poor Clare Nuns have used a loose fitting, open fronted brown cape without hood for the same number of years.

The *choir cape* takes its name from the section of the chancel of the church known as 'the choir', the place where monks and nuns historically gathered together for the celebration of the liturgies of the Church.

Chorale Guida the title of a temporary ad hoc choir assembled at the Vatican comprising volunteers from the public, seminaries, universities and religious communities of Rome. It is called into service on great feasts as a way to supplement the Sistine Choir which serves liturgies at the Vatican and as a way to 'guide' (thus its title) the congregation's responses. When Mass is held inside the basilica this choir is usually found behind the High Altar in the pews in front of the Altar of the Chair.

chorbishop the title granted to certain prelates in both the Oriental Rites of the Roman Catholic Church and in various Orthodox Churches. In the Orthodox communion the title sometimes carries the episcopal dignity. For the Catholic Church the title is used in various Oriental Rites (particularly in the Maronite Rite) in the same way that the title of "Monsignor" or "Honorary Canon" is conferred in the Latin Rite. In some instances, chorbishops of the Catholic Church may confer what was once called minor orders, today known as the offices of Acolyte, Lector and Candidate for Holy Orders. They most often may wear some of the episcopal insignia and vesture, such as mitre, pectoral cross or icon, and they may sometimes carry the crozier just as Protonotaries Apostolic use to do in the Latin Rite, but these privileges in no way elevate the chorbishop to the episcopal dignity. This class of prelate is known in Latin as the *chorepiscopi.*

chrism the special oil used by the church comprising a mixture of pure virgin olive oil and balsam and used by bishops and priests at baptism, confirmation and holy orders. It is also used for the consecration of new churches, chapels, and shrines and also to consecrate a new chalice and paten and ciborium. Traditionally only a bishop consecrates with the holy chrism.

chrismarium the place inside a cathedral or church where the sacrament of Confirmation was traditionally conferred. This place took its name from the ornate vessel that held the holy oil of Chrism used in this sacrament. This term is still applied to the chapels, or side altars, of great cathedrals dedicated as repositories for the diocese's blessed sacramental oils.

Christmas the formal and most solemn liturgical celebration commemorating the birth of Christ now reserved for the twenty-fifth day of December. Originally, the church did not set a specific day aside for this celebration. Some regions celebrated Christ's birth on the Epiphany, most especially the Greeks and the Sicilians, while others did not celebrate it at all. During the pontificate of Pope Marcellino (AD296-304) Rome began to recognize the feast on the twenty-fifth of December in an attempt to incorporate Roman pagans into the church that likewise celebrated winter feasts at that time. Fifty years hence, Emperor Constantine recognized the earlier pope's edict and encouraged Pope Julius I (AD 337-352) to foster this commemoration in December. The word, Christmas, comes from the Old English meaning 'Christ's Mass' as a special Mass was celebrated on the 25th December once the feast was fixed on the liturgical calendar. The Romans referred to this day by the Latin title of *Nativitas Domini* (the birth, or nativity, of the Lord) but by the fourteenth century began to adapt the slang, *Natale,* as well. Today, the liturgical life of the Church extends Christmas for a period of eight days known as the *Octave of Christmas* which does not begin officially until the Vigil Mass one Christmas Eve and which extends to the feast of the Baptism of the Lord.

church (a) a term that denotes a family of believers, such as in general usage 'the Christian Church' which means all believers, or in more specific geographical usage 'the Church of Toronto' meaning only those faithful belonging to the Archdiocese of Toronto. Both canon law and the *Catechism of the Catholic Church* formalize this term in accordance with the laws and theology of the Roman Catholic Church; (b) the term applied to a building set aside for Divine Worship. In the Roman Catholic Church there may be found several types of 'churches': the parish church, a chapel, a shrine, an oratory, etc. The parish church is the canonical presence of the diocese within a set geographical border and is intended as the spiritual home for the faithful within that territory. A pastor or a rector heads it. A chapel is a place of prayer open to all the faithful whereas an oratory is reserved for a few and could best be described as a private chapel.

Churches, Eastern and Western the Christian world has been divided by both natural geography and along political lines since the middle of the fifth century. This circumstance differs from later theological and ecclesial schisms. The Western Churches comprise the Roman Catholic Church and all of its entities (Rites) throughout the world as well as all of the denominations that broke with Rome at the time of the Protestant Reformation. The Eastern Churches comprise all of those denominations that gravitate towards the former Constantinople (Istanbul) including all members of the Orthodox family as well as far distant churches such as the Armenians and the Copts as well as numerous heretical groups such as the Jacobites and Nestorians that linger on today in one form of church body or another. This is difference is categorized as a political division as the split between the two came with the division of the Roman Empire into the more powerful Eastern half based at Constantinople and the weaker, older half remaining at Rome

In terms of the geographical division, the line of demarcation begins in the Baltic running southward through Poland down the Vistula River to the Danube and out to the Adriatic. Those peoples to the east of this division traditionally have looked to Constantinople and those to the west to Rome. The ancient and most honored Eastern Rites of the Roman Catholic Church are not separated from Rome and the west in terms of this geo-political categorization but rather form a part of the greater Roman Catholic Church.

churching a non-sacramental liturgical practice in place prior to the Second Vatican Council (1965) known also as the 'churching of mothers' or the 'churching of women' which was the formal welcome back into the church of a mother after she had properly recovered from the birth of her child and after the baptism of the child had taken place. Only women within a valid state of marriage and those that have had their baby baptized into the Catholic Church could take part. This custom developed in the second century in honor of a similar Hebrew custom at which proper thanks to God were given after a live and safe birth.

ciborium the sacred vessel used as a receptacle of consecrated Hosts to be used for the Holy Communion of the people. The name derives from the Latin, *cibus,* meaning 'food'. The ciborium long mimicked the design of the chalices used in the church but today may be found in many artistic styles. Like the chalice, whatever the style of the design, the interior of the ciborium must be worked in gold or should be heavily gold plated. Until 1965, when the ciborium contained consecrated Hosts, it was always veiled in satin or silk usually made of white or gold to symbolize the Sacred Presence within the vessel.

cincture the term used for the belt or cord that binds the waist in sacred vesture, for the habits of religious men, and for the garb of nuns. In terms of the habit of nuns and religious women, some orders also refer to the *cincture* of their habits as a *girdle.*

cincture, conventual the cord or girdle used by various orders of nuns to encircle the waist. It was most frequently made of white hemp and bore knots representing the vows taken by each particular order—typically poverty, chastity, and obedience. Some conventual cinctures, however, were made of wool and were worked in various colors—black, blue, scarlet or pink, and some (especially the communities founded in the nineteenth century) added tufts to the cords as well. Attached to the conventual cincture was typically an oversized Rosary.

cipher the formal diplomatic, and/or royal court, usage of the single initial of a public person's Christian name for use on stationary, documents and on seals of office similar to the monogram employed by others in ordinary use. A cipher differs from the monogram in that it is normally presented in 'mirror' form, that is to say that the single initial appears in normal fashion and again in the reverse—each image side by side. This is the case for most but not all initials in the Latin alphabet. Those commonly depicted singularly (that is to say not in mirror/reversed form) are the letters: M · W · X · I· N. A cipher may also be ensigned with the crown, coronet or cap of office or rank and is displayed on all manner of documents and decrees of office in addition to stationary use. The cipher is also used by the Byzantines and so the Greek alphabet is often seen as well.

Clarisses the French and Italian collective term for the Order of Poor Clare Nuns.

clerestory (also known as **celestory)** the space of the upper walls of a cathedral that were left devoid of ornamentation. In ancient European churches the upper walls were made of wood and were whitewashed but otherwise left unadorned. The title comes from the word 'celestial' meaning heavenly.

clergy the collective term applied to persons within Holy Orders consisting of deacons, priests, and bishops.

clergy: black and white in the eastern churches the term *black clergy* is applied to those living in the celibate state, these men donning black vesture as the norm.. The term *white clergy* conversely is applied to the married clergy in these churches as their traditional vesture is either white or light grey to distinguish them from those consecrated to the celibate state.

cleric a person ordained into holy orders in the office of deacon, priest or bishop.

college the English title for the Latin *collegium* which in the church refers to a society or body of incorporated persons for a common purpose. In the church examples of such bodies would be the Sacred College of Cardinals or the College of Bishops (referring to all of the world's Catholic bishops together in unison). From this concept later developed the same title for bodies of important learning.

cloister a secluded enclosure attached to churches, cathedrals, and monasteries reserved for solitude and prayer and reflection. It is usually covered. It is also a term applied to the place where nuns in solemn pontifical vows reside (known officially as the *Holy Cloister).*

Co-adjutor an official, typically an archbishop or bishop, assigned to a sitting archbishop or bishop as an assistant with rights to succession to his see when the sitting ordinary retires, dies, or is removed for another reason. Some *co-adjutors* are granted full powers while others are limited until the day they actually succeed to the diocese. The only episcopal office in the church not permitted a co-adjutor is that of the Bishop of Rome. Pope Pius IV so decreed this law on 19 November 1561 but the concept of forbidding a co-adjutor to a pope was accepted as early as the third century. No such appointment was ever made. It is the Vicar General for Rome that performs episcopal functions in the pope's name and this official has no rights to succession to the See of Rome or to the papacy, in the same way that most co-adjutor bishops succeed their residential ordinary. In fact, the Vicar General for Rome, along with nearly all other Vatican officials, looses his positions at the death of the pope.

coif the tight fitting white headdress made of linen that enclosed the head of women religious, typically open only at the face, and upon which was attached either the veil or some other structural device that created a unique habit headdress design for each order or community. Some orders referred to this garb as the *wimple* and some older communities, such as the Sisters of Saint Benedict (as seen in the movie *The Sound of Music*) donned a coif that was heavily plaited. This task was accomplished by each nun learning how to hand-sew hundreds of overlying creases into this garb, a practice that was required after each washing.

collar, conventual the heavily starched white cloth used by various orders of nuns and communities of religious women to encircle the neck and to cover the breast. This garb was intended as both protection of the nun's virtue, by covering the breast, and to further identify each community by the distinctness of their habit. In time, some communities began to replace the starched linen with acetate.

collar, Roman a white linen or acetate collar that completely surrounds the neck of a priest or bishop and which is worn with either the black *cassock,* the *choir cassock*, or with a vest and clerical suit. Sometimes the *Roman collar* is only partly visible, sometimes only a mock version is used as an insert to the tab collar shirt now preferred by clerics.

The *Roman collar* was popularized in the nineteenth century at Rome and thereafter became the style identifying Roman Catholic clergy. Before this time, a variety of cloth collars and scarves were used by priests and in France, a colored collar with two tails that dropped onto the chest was preferred.

collegiate cathedral the correct title of a cathedral of a diocese that has attached to it a chapter of canons.

collegiate church the correct title for a non-cathedral, non-basilica church of some import that has had a chapter of canons attached to it.

colobium sindonis a long, sleeveless linen garb which is derived from the liturgical alb and which is open on both sides and edged in lace and which is used in the coronation rites for (initially) Catholic sovereigns beginning with Charlemagne in AD 800 and later by all Christian kings. The last known usage of this liturgical garment was for the Anglican coronation rites for Elizabeth II in 1952. The striking similarity to the alb of bishops and cardinals suggests the ecclesial link between them and the anointed king or queen.

colonnade a row of columns, usually covered by an arcade or roof.

columbarium a place, very similar to a mausoleum, exclusively for the placement of the ashes of those who have been cremated. Today, many parishes have erected elaborate marble or wooden columbaria inside their churches as a means to assure a blessed final resting place for cremated remains. In so doing, these churches have also found a means of raising funds for the repair and refurbishment of these older edifices as the funds generated by the purchase of space in the columbarium can be substantial.

column a supporting device that is round, made of stone, bronze, or wood, sometimes carved or decorated, comprising base, shaft and capital. The most typical design types in Church architecture are the Doric, Ionic, Corinthian, Tuscan, and Salomonic columns. The Salomonic design, employing ornate twisting motives, was used most commonly for the exterior, particularly in cloister design, although a form of the Salomonic design was found in the white marble columns used in the high altar of the Constantinian Basilica c.A.D. 400 (the original Vatican Basilica) and was later mimicked in bronze by Bernini for the famous baldachino in the current basilica at the Vatican.

commemoration of the dead the ritual, or prayerful sequence, within the canon of the Mass at which time the celebrant inserts the names of those amongst the dead to be remembered and at which time he invites the faithful to silently do the same. This custom began by decree of Pope Saint Gregory the Great (AD 590-604) who ordered the insertion of the names of certain saints into the canon of the Mass.

commemoration of the living the ritual, or prayerful sequence, within the canon of the Mass at which time the priest invites the faithful to pray silently for those living persons to be remembered within the Mass.

Communion of the faithful the custom of placing the Eucharist onto the tongues of the faithful receiving it began by order of Pope Gregory the Great in AD 600. Before this time, the Eucharist consisted of large pieces of consecrated loaves and it was taken in the hand. After it was consumed, the Communicant then was presented the chalice for consumption of the Precious Blood. The return to Communion in the hand came about after the liturgical renewals in the post-Vatican II era. Pope Benedict XVI accommodates those wishing to take the Eucharist in the hand while Pope John Paul II preferred not to do so.

Communion paten the seldom-seen sacred vessel similar to a round plate with a wooden or bone handle used until the present era under the chin of the recipient of Holy Communion so that if the Eucharist were to fall from the hands of the priest, it would be retrieved with proper decorum. After Vatican Council II, the Communion paten fell out of favor although it was never abolished. In Vatican liturgies, the Papal Master of Ceremonies has lately taken to using the inverted lid of the ciborium for this purpose.

conclave a phrase from the Latin, *cum clavis,* meaning 'with key' and which translates in modern usage to 'a locked gathering' at which all of the cardinals of the church under age 80 gather at the Vatican to elect the next pope. The term is also applied to the election of the Prince-Grand Master of the Order of Malta when the electors of the order gather in Rome to elect the next head of that Hospitaller order of knighthood.

concordat a formal treaty with full diplomatic standing between the Holy See and the government of a nation-state, typically a nation with an overwhelmingly Roman Catholic population. A concordat mainly addresses ecclesial standing in that country, offering the Catholic Church certain special privileges.

confessor a cleric who is appointed for the purpose of administering the sacrament of Reconciliation (Confession) to a specific person or class of persons, or one who makes himself available for the faithful for the same purpose.

Confessio the open space at the foot of the papal High Altar in St. Peter's Basilica, which leads down into the crypt area where the apostle was laid to rest in the first century. This open space and staircase was repeated in numerous baroque churches in the seventeenth century where a saint had been laid to rest beneath the church's altar.

confraternities the title for special organizations or societies founded by popes or bishops under the terms of the law of the church for the purpose of good and pious works of one type or the other. Such groups are entitled to enjoy the funds and properties granted to it or bequeathed to it through time and as such can amass great wealth. When a confraternity is permitted to join with another of common purpose these groups are granted the title of *arch- confraternity*. Membership is voluntary but is a lifetime commitment. In Europe, membership in many confraternities is a source of tremendous family pride and honor with membership in some families spanning across several centuries. Each is bound by its own constitutions and canonical authorities govern each. Most maintain a distinct, centuries old costume marking membership in the confraternity. Most of the earlier, Italian, Spanish, French and Portuguese societies still maintain these costumes—some resembling the ominous garb of the Ku Klux Klan organization that has terrorized parts of the United States fro generations as this spurious group imitated the confraternity habits when it self-created in the nineteenth century.

Examples of the more important of these special societies are the Archconfraternity of the Holy Spirit, of Holy Mary of the Divine Assistance, of Saint Rocco, of the Holy Stigmata, of Saint Crisogono, of Our Lady of Mount Carmel, of Saint Lucy of the Gonfalon, of Saint Francis de Paul, of Prayerful Death, of Saint Felix, of Saint Catherine of Siena, etc. There are also modern examples of these pious societies. Best known amongst these are the Confraternity of the Holy Name of Jesus, which was formally erected as the Confraternity of the Most Holy Name of God and of Jesus and the Confraternity Opus Sanctorum Angelorum and the Confraternity of the Precious Blood.

consecrated life the term for persons that have entered a form of religious life by taking the evangelical counsels of chastity, poverty and obedience. There are two avenues within the structure of the church that this life may be undertaken: the secular institutes or the religious institutes. Well-known samples of Institutes of Consecrated Life are the mendicant orders, the monastic orders, the Canons Regular, and the Clerics Regular.

consistory an assembly of all the cardinals of the Church who are present in Rome. Oftentimes, a pope summons every cardinal to Rome for this purpose. Originally, these assemblies were used to actually govern the Church but as it grew, the establishment of an actual government of the Church, known now as the *Roman Curia*, was required and these infrequent assemblies became occasions where special decisions were made or when the reigning pontiff solemnly announced a new initiative for the Church.

There are three types of these assemblies the *secret, semi-secret,* and *public consistory.* Only cardinals may be present with the pope in *secret consistory.* Cardinals, bishops, and the Papal Court are included in the *semi-secret consistory.* All other churchmen and the laity are welcome at the *public consistory.*

Today, the pope informs the cardinals of new nominations to the *Scared College* in *secret consistory* but these new members of the College of Cardinals are installed later in *public consistory.* The finances of the Church are also discussed in *secret consistory,* which might better be served if called the *private* or *closed consistory.*

cord a cincture or belt made of rope used by religious orders of both men and women. Oftentimes this *cord* includes knots in specific places that represent the vows that these religious made at the time of profession. Today, these cords typically include knots representing the vows of *poverty, chastity,* and *obedience.*

cornette (also known as **cornet**) the headdress of the Daughters of Charity of Saint Vincent de Paul and a few other communities of religious women founded in Brittany. This caplet was typical of widowed women in this region of northern France in the sixteenth century when this community was founded. It took the place of the veil common to most orders of women religious. The cornette was made of heavily starched square-cut linen and through the use of special irons and patterns took a swan-like bonnet form that was attached to multiple-plaited white cap that was, in turn, attached to a chignon (hair bun) at the back of each sister's head. The sisters could not go out in inclement weather as water or snow would cause it to collapse. This community abandoned this distinct headdress in favor of a short blue veil after Vatican II, so that the sisters could drive automobiles which before the change the were unable to do, but they no longer use this alternate headdress as part of their habit.

cornu from the Hebrew word for horn, the name for the four corners of fixed altar, almost always carved in an ornamental fashion, which came into the Catholic Church from the ancient Hebrew temple altars of sacrifice where four 'horns' were fastened to the corners of the altar. From this Hebrew term, by way of Catholic usage, comes the modern word "corner".

Corpus Christi the feast that commemorates the Body of Christ in the form of the Holy Eucharist. As the actual historical event of the institution by Christ of the Holy Eucharist took place within the period we now call Holy Week, Pope Urban IV declared a special feast outside the Lenten and Easter period in 1264. This day has ever since included the celebration of the Eucharist, various forms of Eucharistic adoration, and solemn processions expressing the devotion of the faithful to the Blessed Sacrament of Catholics the world over. In Rome, this feast bears the alternate name, Corpus Domini, (the body of the Lord) and is solemnly commemorated by a procession from the Cathedral-Basilica of Saint John Lateran to the Basilica of Saint Mary Major on the Esquiline Hill led by the reigning pope, the cardinals present in Rome and the entire Papal Chapel. In the last years of his life, when debilitated by infirmity,

Pope John Paul II rode in procession in a special mobile shrine, a practice that Pope Benedict XVI has continued.

cotta a longer version of the surplice made of bleached cotton and usually without adornment.

cowl the part of a monk or mendicant's habit that most resembles a hood. Also found on the *choir cape* of some orders of men. In some orders, the *cowl* also includes a mantle that covers the upper breast and shoulders.

crèche the French word describing the Nativity Scene erected during Christmas throughout the Christian world. The term translates to 'crib' and refers to the recreation of the scriptural depiction of the Holy Family finding refuge in a cave or stable in Bethlehem during Herod's enforced census that coincided with the birth of the Savior. Tradition has it that it was Francis of Assisi that used the recreation of the Birth of Christ at Christmas in 1260 in order to teach the rudiments of the faith to ignorant peasants. The custom spread with the rise of the Franciscan family and in short order reached every corner of the world, becoming the most important non-liturgical symbol for the feast of Christmas. The typical crèche includes figures of the Holy Family as well as angels, shepherds, barnyard animals and the Magi. In southern Italy, modern crèches oftentimes include hundreds of figures commemorating the entire village of Bethlehem as well as all those representing persons there for the required census. For hundreds of years the custom dominated Christmas celebrations throughout the world, but the Vatican never embraced it. It was not until the election of Pope John Paul II, Servant of God, in 1978 that a crèche finally found a home at the seat of the Holy See. Pope John Paul II placed a larger-than-life size version outside the basilica in St. Peter's Square and later in his pontificate ordered the erection of a magnificent nativity scene inside the basilica as well.

credence table a small and unobtrusive table placed on the Epistle side of the sanctuary on which is placed all of the vessels and instruments necessary for the exercise of the rite of consecration of the Eucharist at the Mass. Candles and matches are also found on this table which is made of either wood or metal but which should never dominate the sanctuary by its design or appearance.

Creed the Profession of the Faith of the Catholic Church recited at all Masses and during certain other liturgies. It is historically known as the *Nicene Creed* as the canons, or formula, of the profession sprang from the Council of Nicaea (AD 325). The Creed first came into use inside the Mass in AD 589 in Spain. At that time it was recited after the conclusion of the Consecration rite but in 1014 Pope Benedict VIII transferred it to its current position within the liturgy, namely after the Gospel. It is omitted at Baptisms within the Mass and on other liturgical occasions when the faithful renew their baptismal promises collectively. Before the reforms of the liturgy, the Creed was also omitted during Masses said on the feasts of martyrs, confessors, and all female saints other than Mary Magdalene and for the BVM. It also was omitted at Requiem Masses in the old liturgy.

The *Apostle's Creed* is a profession of faith so named because it was long believed to be composed by one or more of the original Twelve at the first Pentecost. It was originally the profession required of converts to the faith at their ritual baptisms as this abbreviated form of profession only included the dogma required to be accepted in the church. Later it came into general usage throughout the church but never was intended to replace, or to serve alternately with, the Nicene Creed.

cremains the official term for the cremated remains of a baptized member of the church. The church forbids the storage or display of cremains in the home or other private place and requires that they be promptly and formally deposited in blessed ground or in the sea. Those who wish to have the cremains of a loved one placed in the sea, must do so in a sealed urn. Catholic ashes are forbidden to spread ashes of a baptized person openly at sea.

Cross, Way of also known as the Stations of the Cross, this sacramental of the church is performed by the faithful by meditating upon the fourteen images of Christ's last journey up the Via Delorosa in Jerusalem. It is formally known as the Way of the Cross in commemoration of the events of the Passion and Death of Jesus Christ. The alternate term, Stations of the Cross, came to us once the custom of following the Way of the Cross began inside church buildings were plaques, or stations, were fixed to the walls, one for each Passion event, so that the people could more easily understand the theological nature of this devotion. Originally, the Way of the Cross was an actual pilgrimage to the Holy Land wherein Europeans traveled to Jerusalem despite great danger to visit the sights of the actual events in Christ's life and death. Once the Muslim invasions made this impossible, symbolic pilgrimages began and in time each church was fixed with the plaques commemorating Jesus' last journey up the Via Delorosa.

crossing the place where two arms of the church join, usually the place where the chancel begins. In baroque Roman architecture this place where the two arms join is also the site of the *Confessio.*

cross vault the space where two opposing vaults within a ceiling join.

crown cardinal the title of a cardinal in past ages nominated to the Sacred College by kings rather than by a pope, a prerogative permitted Catholic monarchs by the popes during the fifteenth to the mid-nineteenth centuries for political reasons. Historic examples of such appointments include Cardinals Wolsey, Richelieu and Mazarin.

crucifer the person, either lay or ecclesiastic, charged with carrying the processional cross in formal liturgies.

crucifix a cross, typically in the Latin style with a shorter transverse arm than the longer vertical portion, on which appears the *corpus,* or body, of Christ. Today the body of Christ is sometimes depicted as vested in the arraignment of the Resurrection symbolizing the completion of the Triduum events—Passion, Death, and Resurrection of Jesus Christ. There can be no crucifix without the body of Christ in some form upon it. The name derives from two Latin words, *cruci* and *fixus,* which translates to 'fixed to a cross.' More ancient crucifix examples include the 'title' which is the plaque bearing the title "Jesus of Nazareth King of the Jews (INRI) which was fixed there as a mockery during the three hours that

Christ hung upon the Cross at Calvary. Many older crucifix also bear the death head symbolism—the crossed bones and skull representing Golgotha. The theology of the church relates that Christ on the Cross at Golgotha rises out of the death of Adam, thus the inclusion of the death symbolism.

cruets the glass, clay, mosaic, or metal flasks used on the altar to contain the water and the wine to be used at the consecration of the Mass. Before 1965 it was mandatory for these to be made of glass to clearly distinguish the water from the wine but today various materials are permitted. Traditionally a matching basin and a purificator are kept with the cruets for the rite of *Lavabo,* or washing of hands.

crypt a highly decorative place in the church where high-ranking prelates is buried and where other important dignitaries are sometimes laid to rest. Most former popes rest in crypts beneath churches found in Italy, and after the seventeenth century, most commonly beneath St. Peter's in the Vatican. Cardinals are traditionally buried in either their titular church in Rome or in their home cathedral. Archbishops and bishops rest in the crypts beneath their cathedrals and pastors sometimes in crypts in front of their parishes.

Monks and nuns are traditionally laid to rest in crypt chapels, that is to say a small chapel devoted to the tombs of the monastery's members, religious men and women and secular clergy are buried in cemeteries. Important lay people, especially state personages such as royalty, have also been buried in crypts within the most prominent churches in their realms. All others are relegated by Church custom to consecrated ground in local cemeteries.

crypt markers the Christian custom of marking the graves of beloved dead with both a symbol of Christianity and the deceased's name. Originally a pagan custom, today Christians everywhere mark their lifelong membership in the Church on their crypt marker. Ancient Rome only buried the most prominent of its citizens but did so with great honor and distinction. The poor were burned. The graves of the Roman emperors were elaborate temples; those of the senators monuments to their greatness.

Once Constantine the Great legalized Christianity in the fourth century, Catholics also began to build monuments to their dead. Christian emblems replaced pagan symbols and the cross and other identifiable monograms began to appear in consecrated ground owned by the Church. Today, Catholics place crypt-markers, also known as *tombstones,* on the graves of their beloved dead to identify them as Christian believers, as followers of Christ as much as they do to identify where their loved ones may be buried.

cubilia the space, known also as a vault, where the bodies of prelates are laid to rest inside a crypt of a cathedral or in a monastery of monks or nuns where the members' remains are placed after death.

cum jure successionis the Latin term which translates to *with rights to succession* and which is applied to the appointment of those co-adjutore bishops and archbishops granted permission to succeed to the See at the death or retirement of the incumbent.

cupola the term generally applied to a small dome. In the Italian language, however, the term "cupola" also applies to domes of all sizes, including Michelangelo's dome atop St. Peter's Basilica.

curate the cleric on the parish level that assists the pastor or rector of the place. From the Latin the term curate translates to 'care-taker' symbolizing the assisting role that the junior priest plays in parish life. Today, most priests holding this position prefer the alternate title 'parochial vicar' to that of curate.

Curia Romana the Italian title for the term 'Roman Curia' meaning the government of the Catholic Church; a collective term used to denote the various bodies and organizations comprising the pope's administration at Rome. Comprising the curia as a whole this title is applied to the papal secretariat (the pope's personal office), the Secretariat of State, the sacred congregations, tribunals, councils, commissions, councils, prefectures, secretariats and bureaus as well as special institutions such as the Pontifical Swiss Guard regiment and the various papal academies, all in their own way responsible for the work of the church at Rome and across the world.

custos the Latin term that translates to 'custodian' and which is used in two ways within the church. The first is to designate the person who cares for any parish church other than the Sacristan who cares for the sacristy and all items found there. The *custos* in this case is a position of housekeeping inside the church and may be a male or female. The second use of this title is applied to a position within the Franciscan order and is held by a priest in Jerusalem who serves as the senior most official of the order in the Holy Land, in particular the priest assigned to assure that all of the great Catholic churches in the Holy Land are protected and preserved.

daughter the official term used by the church to identify a jurisdiction that once belonged to another such as a *daughter-diocese* in which case a new diocese is created out of the territory of an existing see, or a *daughter-house* in which case a new convent or monastery is formed in a different place because the original house grew beyond its physical limitations.

deacon the first of the major orders comprising deaconate, priesthood and the episcopacy. The title comes from the Greek, *diakonos*, meaning a servant or attendant. Saint Paul, in the first letter of Timothy 3:8, refers to them as servants in the church. In the post-conciliar era, the Office of Deacon was returned fully to the Church with the continuation of the Transitional Deaconate (those men continuing on to priesthood) and a recognition of the Permanent Deaconate (those laymen seeking ordination but who are of the married state of life and thus cannot move on to priesthood or those that do not wish to move on to the presbyterate).

deaconess an ancient title from the earliest church accorded to widows who came to the altar to assist in the preparation of the church for the sacraments. It was not a rank or office in holy orders or an institution formalized by the church as some have claimed. Some have claimed that the title was assumed by wives and widows of men who had been ordained to the diaconal office but there is no proof in the ancient law that this was so. What is known is that the *deaconesses* of the early period were women entrusted with charitable works—mainly with the care of the orphaned. In several Protestant churches, the office of deaconess took on a more formalized existence in the middle nineteenth century when women seeking to live in common and to undertake holy work were given this title in a similar fashion to women religious in the Catholic Church being referred to as nuns.

dean the English language title for the head of a chapter of canons. It is also the ecclesiastical title for a diocesan priest who has been appointed by his bishop to oversee the priests and parishes of a set territory within that diocese. Sometimes this territory mimics civil geographical divisions, such as a county; sometimes it does not mimic any territorial boundaries at all. In both instances, this territory is known as a *deanery*. Deans have certain canonical privileges as well as privileges of precedence and in ecclesial heraldry as well.

decretals the title in Latin for a decision issued by a pope or one of the heads of the offices of the Roman Curia in the pope's name. A decretals is technically a letter addressing a matter of discipline to be imposed but in recent time this title has also been applied to all decisions put to a pope or to the Vatican in order to heal a dispute.

demotion the term used by the church when a jurisdiction is downgraded in classification. An example of a demotion would be the Diocese of Funchal in Madeira. This Portuguese island dependency in the Atlantic Ocean was first erected as a diocese in 1514. It was subsequently elevated to an archiepiscopal see in 1533 but was returned to the rank of diocese (i.e. demotion) in 1551. Another example of this procedure would be Avignon in France, which was first erected as a diocese in c. A.D. 540. It was elevated to the status of Metropolitan Archdiocese in 1475 but was demoted again in 1801 to the status of diocese. In 1822 it was again promoted to Metropolitan Archdiocese only to be demoted to (non-metropolitan) Archdiocese in the reorganization of the dioceses of France in 2002.

Deo gratias a short phrase or acclamation used in the Church as an act of gratitude for some supposed grace received from God. It is still commonly used throughout Europe on such occasions and translates into English as *thanks be to God.* The phrase is also used within the liturgy of the Mass when the Mass is celebrated in Latin.

deuil blanc a French term that translates loosely to 'white morning' which refers to the use of pure white attire by widows in some Latin nations most notably by royal and noble widows. The custom was more common in the Middle Ages than in the modern era but two recent royal widows preferred this form of mourning dress to the more traditional black: Queen Fabiola of Belgium at the death of her husband King Baudoin and for a brief time Britain's Queen Elizabeth, the Queen Mother after the death of George VI in 1952 and the Dutch royal family adopted it as well at the deaths of Queen Wilhelmina and Queen Juliana.

diaspora the title given to all of the nations around the Mediterranean basin where the Jews of Palestine took refuge particularly after the rise of Islam but even prior to this period in history. Technically, the first *diaspora,* which is from the Greek meaning 'exile,' took place during the Babylonian captivity of the Jews in the eight century before Christ.

diocese the termed used by the church to designate jurisdictional territory, typically governed by a bishop. The word "diocese" comes to us from the Greeks, *dioikesis,* meaning a government or administration. This is the fundamental form of local church. Today, for fraternal and administrational purposes, several dioceses are gathered together to form an ecclesiastical province. Each diocese is independent and the bishop of each see enjoys full powers of administration, however, the largest, or historically most important, diocese within this province is given the status of "first amongst equals" and is known as an *Archdiocese* and is typically governed by an *archbishop.*

Dioecesis Urbs seu Romana the official Latin title for the Diocese of Rome.

discalced the Latin term meaning 'barefooted'. In the Church this title has been extended to those communities of religious who not only wear sandals rather than shoes but which have been reformed in one degree or another from the original foundation of that order, as in the case of the *Discalced Carmelites.*

disciple a title from the Latin, *discipulus, meaning 'follower.' For Christian believers this is the title of all of those who came to follow Christ, both during His lifetime and after his Crucifixion, other than the Apostles who bore a separate, unique title to set them apart from all others.*

dispensation the act of forgiving or removing obligation of a specific law or mandatory custom or practice. A pope may grant a dispensation to the entire world or parts of it because of his universal jurisdiction but he may never grant dispensation from what is known to be the law of God. Cardinals may offer the dispensation universally or to large regions on behalf of the expressed wish of a pope but may not do so of their own accord. The archbishops and bishops may grant dispensations within their own jurisdiction so long as they do not come in opposition to expressed law of the Church. The bishops tend to have the right to dispense with acts of their own or of their predecessors in that place but they cannot act on a universal law without Rome's permission. There are several forms of the act of dispensation each granted for specific reasons or causes. Popes for instance may change the length of time of the pre-Eucharistic fast (which Paul VI imposed changing it from 12 hours to 60 minutes prior to the receipt of Holy Communion). Bishops may offer a dispensation to not attend Sunday Mass when the weather is too severe for the faithful of a given place to journey outside) and dispensations can be granted for a Catholic to marry a non-Catholic within a valid marriage or for a seminarian to be ordained without the normal extensive training required of candidates.

Divine Office the original title of the *Liturgy of the Hours*, the rotation of prayers, hymns, canticles and readings sung or continuously prayed throughout the church.

dogma the collective term used by the Christian churches when speaking of the fundamental beliefs and theological laws of a given church. The title comes from the Greek originally from a phrase meaning 'a collection of sacred writings' but today refers more to our beliefs as a Church either collectively as a body of philosophical and theological tenants or as individual laws. A dogma can be said to encompass one or more fundamental truths pertaining to the faith. The study of the fundamental truths of the faith is known as *dogmatic theology.*

dome an evenly curved vault that is mounted on top of a circular drum that provides it with its ultimate shape.

dominiative the canonical title applied to the powers of jurisdiction of the superior of a religious house over its members (subjects) under his authority. This power is applied to the way of life within the house and to power to delegate and disperse property.

domino the lightweight white veil sometimes worn under the heavier black, brown, or gray veil worn by nuns that presents an overall white appearance around the face for these orders' habits. The *domino* is also the veil used by novices although this name is not always applied to it in this instance. The *domino* is also the term once applied to the prelatial hoods worn by European canons.

Dominus Apostolicus the most common form of address of the popes from the sixth century until the late Renaissance, early Baroque, periods translating to 'Most Apostolic Lord' and the predecessor of the modern form of address— 'Most Holy Father.'

Dominus Vobiscum the Latin phrase for the opening to universal prayer of the church meaning: *The Lord be With You.*

dossal curtain the title of the elaborately decorative silk, satin, or damask brocade clothe used behind the *reredos* or high altar as a background device. It came into existence out of necessity, in place of the rare tapestries originally used for the same purpose. Some churches are designed in such a way that the dossal curtain may be changed for every change in the liturgical season; green, purple, red, white or gold. When this is not possible, the color and pattern selected for a permanent dossal curtain may be selected to match the interior design of the particular church employing it.

drum the thick, round supporting wall at the base of a large dome. It may or may not be pierced by windows or ornamentation.

dulia the proper Latin term for the act of veneration of the saints.

duomo the Italian term for cathedral, deriving from the architectural feature of the dome surmounting most great Italian cathedrals. A similar term in German, *Dom,* is used for the same purpose.

Durham Rite A combination of the Celtic and the French liturgical rites used in and near Durham. The bishop of this historic English see held the title of count-palatine. To recognize this unique high office a diadem was placed at the base of the bishop of Durham's mitre.

Durante munere a Latin term meaning "for the time or duration" which applies to a post or title granted a churchman only during the time he holds a specific post.

Easter the principle feast on the Christian liturgical calendar and the fulfillment of the Old Testament. Easter commemorates the Passion, Death, and Resurrection of Our Lord Jesus Christ. Known also as Easter Sunday because the historical Resurrection of Christ took place on the Sunday morning within the Jewish Passover. In Greek it was known as *pascha*, which came into modern linguistics from the Hebrew *pesach* meaning to pass over. From this translation the term came into ancient Latin and all the modern Latin derivative languages have maintained this title ever since. In Italian it is rendered as *pascha,* in French *pâques,* and in Spanish *pascua.* The English term for this feast comes to us from the Old Anglo-Saxon word, *eâstron,* a name for the spring goddess *Estre.* The feast for this German mythological goddess was extremely important in pagan Germany but once Christianized the Anglo-Saxon peoples transferred the title of the spring festival to the new Christian commemoration.

During the first centuries of the Christian era, the church celebrated the commemoration of the Resurrection each Sunday. But soon the church began to set a specific date to commemorate the Resurrection once a year, changing it many times throughout the first four centuries with some variance by locality. But by the pontificate of Leo I "the Great" (AD 440-461) the church finally set aside one specific day to commemorate the actual historic Resurrection, thereafter celebrating it on the first Sunday after the full moon of the spring equinox. This was the day that the precise Hebrew calendar records as the day Jesus rose from the dead. As this is the central event in the Christian year, all other seasons are fixed around it.

Easter fire, historical origin of the ancient custom of lighting bonfires on the mountain tops across Central Europe during the pagan festival of spring. The fires had to be created anew, not taken from existing flames, which signified the victory of the life that spring brings over death found in the coldness of winter. In Christian terms, this belief was translated into the hope that the Resurrection brings all mankind. Thus, the custom of the spring bonfire was introduced as the Easter Fire in AD 450. Today this ancient ritual takes place inside every Catholic church the world-over at the Vigil Mass on Holy Saturday evening.

Ember days a custom that came into the Church from the pagans of Rome who celebrated numerous times a year as an act of thanksgiving to the Roman gods for the benefits that came to man at the close of each season of the years. The early church at Rome seeing the benefit for including end of season thanksgiving incorporated the Ember days into the Roman liturgical calendar in the third century. By the sixth century these set-aside days became days of severe fast and repentance so as to remind the faithful what God had given them and why they should be thankful for it. The custom of the Ember Days continued until the modernizations of the liturgical calendar and the customs of the Church after the Second Vatican Council in 1965. These days were traditionally scheduled for Wednesdays, Fridays and Saturdays and fell just after the feast of Santa Lucia (December 13), after Ash Wednesday, and after Pentecost. They were also imposed on those days after the feast of the Exaltation of the Cross in September.

ecclesiastical signatures Church custom designates certain forms and practices in regards to the manner in which prelates of the Church sign documents. The popes sign all documents in a formula that includes the Latin version of his papal name followed by the initials 'P.P' meaning 'pope and pontiff' followed by the Roman numeral designating the number of popes' who bore that name, such as in the case *Johannes P.P.*

XXIII for Pope John XXIII. Cardinals include their title in their signature, appearing after their baptismal name and before their surname. Patriarchs, archbishops, bishops and abbots include a cross before their signature. Abbesses sign their religious, or profession, name along with any title linked to that name. For instance, *Mother Rose of Assisi* (the profession name) *of the Holy Angels* (the title also granted her at profession) to be followed by the title 'abbess'.

emeritus from the Latin "ex" meaning 'without' and 'meritus' meaning 'merit' but which generally translates to 'no longer with standing', the title granted to a person who voluntarily surrenders a post and title due to age, retirement, or ill health. This title is applied to all offices within the church, reserved for those persons formerly enjoying a specific rank or office, but is most commonly seen used for retired bishops who are said to be a 'Bishop Emeritus of the place.' The plural for emeritus is *emeriti.*

The feminine form for emeritus is **emerita.** This title is applied in very rare instances to abbesses elected or installed for life but who retire for health reasons, thus relinquishing their rights and titles before death. The most recent appointment of *Abbess-Emerita* was Mother Angelica whose health made it impossible to continue to govern her monastery in Hanceville, Alabama.

empore the term used to describe a gallery above the nave of a large church. The finest example of this device in the United States are the "galleries" that run high atop the interior walls of the Basilica of the National Shrine of the Immaculate Conception in Washington, DC.

enchiridion the term used by the church for all manner of handbooks. Perhaps the most famous of these is the *Enchiridion Indulgentiarum,* or the Handbook of Indulgences, which sites all of the indulgences granted by the church in all matters ecclesial, liturgical, and devotional.

enclosure, papal the term applied to a cloistered convent or monastery meaning that no one other than a physician, dentist, and Father Confessor may enter the enclosed space where the nuns or monks live. This rule is strictly enforced and only a pope (thus the reference to "papal" enclosure) and a cardinal may enter at will. Even the bishop of the place must seek the permission of the superior of the place to enter and no other person, ecclesiastic or lay, may enter for any reason whatsoever.

eparch the equivalent of a bishop in the Eastern Rites.

eparchy the equivalent of a diocese within the Eastern Rites.

Epiphany officially known as the Solemnity of the Epiphany of the Lord Jesus Christ, a solemn feast and Holy Day of Obligation throughout the Universal Church. This feast is celebrated on the sixth of January and commemorates the manifestation (epiphany) of the Christ Child to the Gentiles. Also known as "Little Christmas" and as the *Theophany*, the Epiphany is symbolized by Christ's manifestation to the Magi. It was the custom during the pontificate of Pope John Paul II, Servant of God, that a number of newly named bishops would be consecrated on this day at Saint Peter's Basilica in the Vatican.

There are actually three official 'epiphany feasts' in the Church. The first is celebrated on the 6th of January celebrating the arrival of the Magi representing the manifestation of the Christ Child. The second is the following Sunday on the feast of the Baptism of the Lord in which John the Baptist identifies the adult Jesus as the Savior. The third takes place the week following the second event on the Sunday after the Baptism of the Lord which is set aside in the liturgical calendar for the revelation of the Wedding Feast at Canaan at which time the Apostles come to know Jesus as the Son of God because of His first miracle converting the water to wine.

episcopacy all things pertaining to the body of bishops. The title used by the Catholic Church in reference to the Office of Bishop. This should not be confused with the Episcopal Church which is the title used in the United States to designate membership in the Anglican Church or Church of England.

episcopi vagantes the Latin term applied to renegade bishops who have been consecrated to this office without the proper canonical credentials and/or permissions and which translates literally to *wandering bishops*. Usually, these so-called bishops are not attached to any one church body other than a small community that forms around them so as to add legitimacy to their episcopal ordination. If an adherent of the Catholic Church at the time of such an act, the priest involved immediately excommunicates himself. The Catholic Church had considered the Lefebvre consecrations in this way. The singular for of this term in Latin would be *episcopus vagans*.

Eucharist from the Greek meaning 'Thanksgiving' the term applied to the Blessed Sacrament at the Holy Sacrifice of the Mass comprising both Body and Blood, Soul and Divinity of Jesus Christ. The Eucharist, or Holy Communion, is both a sacrament and a sacrifice at the same time and is one of the fundamental pillars of the Catholic Church. It was given to the church personally by Christ at the Last Supper. The term 'Eucharist' is often applied as a secondary title for the Mass because of its original Greek meaning but more accurately it should be applied to the Blessed Sacrament within the Mass.

eucharistic salute the term applied to two acts of reverence used to honor the Real Presence of Christ within the Eucharist. The first came into the Church from the ancient Roman Empire wherein soldiers used the placement of a closed right hand over the heart to honor the emperor or other officials of high rank. Christians realized early on that this form of honor could be adapted for Church use and so this once pagan military salute became the proper way to show profound respect for Christ in the Eucharist, particularly at the moment of the two elevations at the consecration of the Mass. The second application of this title is applied to the act of genuflection by all the faithful before the Blessed Sacrament and to the Pontifical Swiss Guard whose officers genuflect within the Mass in a unique form of military salute to the Christ in the Eucharist.

Evangelical Counsels the vows of Chastity, Poverty, and Obedience so called because Christ and the Apostles openly embraced these virtues and because Jesus taught them as we know from the Gospels.

evêque de la cour a French phrase applied to the bishop that the popes would routinely send unofficially to the Catholic royal courts of Europe. As this bishop had no diplomatic standing, and was present at the foreign capital to foster the papacy's spiritual program rather than its political agenda, the host monarch would typically nominate him as one of his senior palatine chaplains. By the time that the Vatican permitted this unofficial post to lapse after the First World War the need for this unofficial listening post had long been superceded by the extremely efficient papal diplomatic corps. In places where full diplomatic standing does still not exist, the descendent of the evêque de la cour, the *Apostolic Delegate,* assumes this posting in the foreign capital.

ex indumentis the title for relics of a saint, or a candidate for sainthood, that comprises parts of the cloth or known personal belongings of that candidate or canonized saint.

exarch whereas an eparch is the equivalent of a diocesan bishop of the Latin Rites within the Eastern Rites of the Catholic Church, the exarch was once much more. The prelate that had enjoyed this rank and title before the 18th century was solely subject to the Patriarch of his rite but to no other. It was a common, but seldom granted, title of both the Eastern Rites of the Catholic Church and of the Eastern Orthodox Churches (not affiliated with Rome in any way). It Latin terms, it could be said that the exarchs of old were a special metropolitan in charge of other metropolitans that than, in turn, control their own bishops. The closest office to these exarch of old in today's Latin Rite would be the 'primate' although the exarchs then exercised more authority than the primates, which are no more than *primus inter pares* in each place.

Today, however, an exarch may be merely a minor bishop, or a prelate that has not been elevated to the office of bishop, and is a very common title within the various Oriental Rites of the Catholic Church. In the modern sense, the exarch is more akin to the Latin Rite's Vicar's Apostolic or Prelate's Apostolic such as in the case of the Greek Melkite exarchate for Argentina; the church there maintaining a real presence but not one large enough to warrant a sitting bishop in that place.. Today there are patriarchal exarchs and archiepiscopal exarchs, each formed according to the rubrics of those titles.

The original concept of the exarch came from the early Byzantine Empire at which time the office was non-ecclesial and more akin to a modern governor-general. The exarch in the Orthodox Churches did not develop in modern terms in the same way as did those in the Roman Catholic Church.

exarchate the territory, or canonical jurisdiction, of an exarch.

ex-cathedral the proper designation for a church that once, but no longer, had been the cathedral of a diocese. To be so called, the cathedral in question must formally have been stripped of its title as the seat of the local bishop. Not to be confused with *ex cathedra* which means something entirely different—the official status of the doctrinal teachings of the local bishop or a pope.

Executor, Apostolic a temporary posting granted by the reigning pope to a specific cleric with the charge of delivering and enforcing a Papal Rescript. When the papal decree is intended for members of a religious order, then the Apostolic Executor is traditionally the superior of that order unless it would be impossible or difficult for him to impose the pope's will. If the rescript is intended for a priest or layperson in a given diocese, then the Apostolic Executor appointed is traditionally the diocesan bishop of that place. If the rescript is intended for a residential bishop alone, then the Apostolic Executor appointed would be either a member of the Sacred College or a high ranking member of the Roman Curia. This title should not be confused with the personage named as legal executor of a deceased pope's Last Will and Testament.

exegesis an act of officially explaining something pertaining to the truths of the faith. It is generally quite extensive in its explanation and it traditionally includes citation of numerous sources for reference so as to reinforce the authenticity of the discourse.

exequial liturgy the burial rites used for funerals of cardinals.

exorcism the formal act or ritual of driving out of Satan, evil spirits, or demons of one possessed by these or by places believed to be dwelling places for them. The ritual is a formalize liturgical rite within the Catholic Church and requires a specially trained priest to perform these rituals under the title of an *exorcist* of the Church.

extern a nun, brother, or monk of a cloistered house that has either been accepted into the house for the sole purpose of serving the external needs of the community, or who has been admitted inside but found the cloistered life to be too oppressive. In either case, the religious lives near or adjacent to the monastery or abbey and is charged with the greeting and care of visitors, the securing of staples for the house, and in modern times, even driving cloistered religious to the physician, hospital, or dentist. Most commonly, the habit of the extern is very similar to those within the cloister but it is differenced so that a clear spiritual and canonical distinction is made.

external forum those conversations and trusts between a bishop, or priest and another cleric, or between a member of the clergy and a member of the laity, that are not protected under the seal of the confessional and can therefore be opened to public scrutiny.

extraordinary form the title applied by the church to the celebration of the Traditional Latin Mass, or Tridentine Mass, in the modern era as encouraged by Pope Benedict XVI. It is referred to as 'extraordinary' because the current form of the Mass, the Novus Ordo instituted after the close of the Second Vatican Council in 1965, remains the 'ordinary' or normal celebration or form of the sacred liturgy of the Catholic Church.

fabrica, ecclesiæ sometimes also rendered as *Fabbrica*, the term applied by the church to the total cost of constructing a new church building and also applied to the period of construction of the same. This term applies to all new church construction projects but is best known also as a department of the Roman Curia—known by the formal name 'the Reverend Fabric of Saint Peter's in the Vatican', which first came into being in the fifteenth century when 'new' Saint Peter's was under construction. The department charged with on-going upkeep and repairs as well as the staffing of the Vatican basilica thereafter took this name.

façade the front of a building, usually ornamented. In the Church the term façade is traditionally reserved for the West Front with the towers and great rose window. In Catholic architecture the façade varies by the historic period so that what is typical to a Romanesque church would not be typical in a French gothic cathedral but these differences reflect changes in style and not the form.

faculties the canonical term for the powers vested in a cleric with the lawful right to perform them such as a priest possessing the faculty to hear confessions, a bishop to ordain, or a deacon to baptize. The new code of canon law speaks of universal faculties according to the given office in Holy Orders, but prior to its promulgation, a cleric had to seek permission from the bishop of a place other than his own in order to exercise the faculties of his ecclesial office.

familiars the term applied to the personal or ecclesial staff of the Holy Father such as his valet, physician or confessor. The private functionaries possess a place of honor and distinction in papal processions and are also considered to be members of the Papal Chapel. The term comes into the church from early monastic life when outsiders boarded within the religious house so as to perform functions not traditionally undertaken by the monks or religious of the place.

fasting a sacrificial or penitential custom by which all persons of a specific age are bound by church law to forego a full diet on proscribed days of the year as a special offering to God and as a means of spiritual purification and preparation. Today the Church requires a full fasting for those in good health between the ages of eighteen and fifty-nine on Ash Wednesday and Good Friday only. The fast has also been modified so that it permits one full meal and two lighter meals, rather than the original concept of a penitential diet of bread and water.

Unlike *abstinence*, which came into the Church in the fourth century, *fasting* as self-sacrifice can be traced to ancient Jewish law. It can be found in the tenants laid down by Moses who demanded a full, or strict, fast on the Day of Atonement. The Old Testament likewise cites Elias's fasting as an example to the Jewish nation as a sound means of reconciliation with the God of Israel. We also know from Sacred Scripture that Jesus, Himself, observed the penitential fast as a rite of self-purification when he entered the desert for forty days, going without substantial food for the duration of his exile there.

The concept of sacrificial *fasting* has changed through the centuries. Until the eighth century, Catholics were required to observe a strict fast from Saturday after sunset until Sunday at sunset. Later, the 'Communion Fast' was relaxed to the period between midnight Saturday until after an individual received the Eucharist the following morning at Sunday Mass. Today, the 'Communion Fast' is set at one hour prior to the receipt of the Blessed Sacrament.

feasts, ecclesiastical the days on the liturgical calendar set aside to honor the historical events in the redemption of mankind, particularly commemorating the events in the life of Christ, His many titles, the titles and events in the life of the Blessed Virgin Mary and the lives of the Apostles, martyrs and saints of the church. Of these days, certain feasts are known as Holy Days of Obligation; days when the whole church celebrates such as Christmas or All Saints Day. The number of these days of obligation, when all Catholics are obliged to attend Mass, differs from nation to nation. Most days of the week now have more than one normal commemoration due to the huge number of proclaimed saints today. In addition, some saints are only commemorated locally rather than being placed on the Universal liturgical calendar.

femorale short lightweight cloth pants, from the waist to below the knees, worn by men in religious life under their habits in place of normal trousers. The *femorale,* which takes its name from the 'femoral bone' are traditionally made in the same color of the habit. Secular clergy in Europe also make use of the *femorale* but elsewhere in the world long pants are worn under the cassock. The pope still wears white *femorale* in place of pants under his white *simar.*

fidei donum translated as 'faithfully given' the term applied to a priest who is loaned to another diocese, typically a mission territory or to a specific race or ethnic group of people in a foreign place, without his becoming incardinated in that place.

First Priest the English language term for the title of the most senior Cardinal-Priest of the Church.

flabellum, Eastern Rite the large fan-like device used to keep insects from the Eucharist and the ministers of the Eucharist which originated in ancient Egypt. The Roman, or papal, flabellum comprised a large fan with ostrich plumes upon a ten-foot long staff. The Eastern Rite made use of a shorter staff upon which was mounted the symbol of the Seraph: the head of a child with three sets (or six individual) wings—two upright, two outreaching, and two downward.

Forty Hours Devotion a Eucharistic devotion begun in Milan in the late sixth century so as to promote a greater reference for Christ in the form of the Blessed Sacrament. Although this was popularized throughout Europe it was never taken up by the Church in the United States until Bishop (now Saint) John Neumann of Philadelphia introduced it throughout his diocese 1853. It has continued every day in a succession of parishes thereafter. From Philadelphia the devotion spread across North America where it is now one of the most popular Catholic devotions. The Forty Hours devotion is quite simple, an opening ceremony, homilies at specific intervals, and a closing ceremony including a procession of the Eucharist within an elaborate monstrance. The faithful are called to come into the church during this continuous forty hour period so that "Jesus will not be alone" and so that continuous prayer and adoration will take place throughout the devotion period.

fra the title of the professed members of the Sovereign Hospitaller Order of Saint John of Jerusalem, of Rhodes and of Malta taken from the Latin *frater* meaning 'brother'. The title precedes the Christian name of the professed member as in the case of the former Grand Master of the order, Fra Matthew Festing.

friar The title of some orders of Religious men, including priests, such as the Augustinians. See also: *Brother, religious.*

friary the home of a group of friars. When a diocese entrusts one of its parishes to the spiritual care of a religious order where the priests refer to themselves as 'friars' the rectory is traditionally referred to as a Friary.

frieze a long expanse of stone used for decoration or epitaphs at the top of a palace or church façade.

frontal, altar an elaborate, artistic cloth or wooden piece that is applied to the front of an altar for decorative purposes. Sometimes these are very rare and valuable artworks in themselves.

funeral dues the title of the fees that canon law permitted a pastor to collect when one of his parishioners died. Of course today this custom is obsolete. Parishes today charge a specific sum which the funeral director pays on behalf of the family (to be reimbursed later) but before the middle of the twentieth century a priest had the right to assess dues based upon the wealth of the deceased. If a parishioner died outside his residence city, and was buried there in place of home, the local pastor could demand one-fourth of the these dues from the pastor of another city who performed the burial rites.

Gallic Rite the liturgical formula which sprang up in France, primarily from the Cluniac monastic monasteries with aspects unique to the French language and culture.

Gamp or **gimp** A white starched linen cloth that was designed to surround the neck, face and head of a nun or religious woman as part of the garb that comprised her religious habit until modern adaptations to religious clothing for women rendered it obsolete. This ensemble could be made to fit loosely as in the case of the mendicant's habits, pleated as in the case of some congregations of Benedictines, or tight fitting as in the case of most of the more modern orders. Only those orders still maintaining traditional habits continue to make use of the *gamp* or *gimp* in their habits. *(See also coif).*

Gaudate or Gaudate Sunday, the third Sunday in the season of Advent taking its name from the first word of the introit of the Mass for this day, Gaudate, which translates to 'Rejoice.' It is also rendered as Gaudete in some places and is known as one of the two Rose or Pink Sundays as vestments of these colors replace the purple common for Advent on this day.

gentilis homo the Latin term for 'gentleman' and used by the church to refer to those laymen serving the pope, cardinals or some archbishops as gentlemen of honor, chamberlains, or aides de camp. The title is rendered in Italian in many instances such as *Gentiluomo di Sua Santità,* or Gentleman of His Holiness, for those that serve the pope in these capacities and simply as *Gentiluomo* for the post of 'Gentleman of the Cardinal-Archbishop of Westminster'.

genuflection a gesture of profound obeisance and respect in which a person drops to his or her right knee in the presence of one of higher office. The *genuflection* was invented in ancient Rome and was used by the Centurions as a mark of respect for senators, generals, caesars and the emperor. The Romans believed that the right side of the body was closer to the operation of the heart muscle, thus their selection of the right knee for the act of genuflection as the most profound gesture of respect possible. The terms comes from the Latin *genu flectere, meaning 'to bend the knee.'*

The infant Church quickly adopted this form of ceremonial deference for reverencing the Blessed Sacrament, a custom that continues today. In time, the Holy Roman emperors desired to implement the *genuflection* as a way to honor their own august person but the popes vehemently objected. Women eventually designed a form of it for use, the *curtsey,* which is still used when greeting royalty. In time, men for royal figures and other high state officials likewise adopted the bow.

Although the liturgical customs of the Church continue to include the act of genuflection for reverencing the Blessed Sacrament, a deep bow has also become popular. *(See also Bow, liturgical).*

Gloria the sequence of the Mass known historically as the "Angelic Hymn' as it is an abbreviated version of the hymn of the angelic choirs above Bethlehem at the birth of the Christ Child. It is sometimes correctly referred to as the "Greater Doxology" from the Greek, which translates to "to speak praise and glory." The Gloria came into the Mass in the second century. It is believed that Pope Telesphorus formally mandated it for Roman use in AD 130.

Good Friday this is the day in the liturgical calendar which the church reserves for the commemoration of the crucifixion of Jesus Christ. It is always set as the Friday in Holy Week, or the Friday prior to the Easter Sunday celebration. It is also the only day of the year when the Eucharist is not celebrated. Good Friday is marked by penitential silence, solemn prayerfulness and the veneration of the Holy Cross.

Good Friday Collection is those moneys collected in all of the Roman basilicas and churches under the control of the Vatican during liturgies held in these churches on Good Friday. These moneys are always sent to the Catholic Church in the Holy Land in special tribute to the faith in Christ's homeland and as a means to keep the faith alive there.

Gospel(s) the term used by the church to signify the historical text of Christ's own words and deeds in narrative form. The term comes from Old English, God-spell, which means to teach God's word. The Gospels are known in Latin as the *Evangelium.* Catholic tradition recognizes four books of the Gospels; those of Matthew, Mark, Luke, and John. As the authors of these works, they are known collectively as the *Evangelists.* In all, there are more than fifty books that have been claimed at one time or the other as being Gospels, and some of churches do recognize some of these as such, but the Catholic Church formally recognizes only the works of the four Evangelists.

Gospeller, the Old English Catholic title for the Deacon of the Word. Now only seen in the Anglican Church but once very much a part of the lexicon of the Catholic Church in the British Isles.

Greek cross a cross design used in church architecture in which the four arms are of equal length.

Greek Rite the liturgical formula used amongst the Byzantine churches in union with Rome. These include: the Albanian Greek Catholic Church, the Belarusian Greek Catholic Church, the Bulgarian Greek Catholic Church, the Byzantine Catholic Church of Croatia and of Serbia, the Greek Byzantine Catholic Church, the Greek Melkite Catholic Church, the Hungarian Greek Catholic Church, the Italo-Albanian Catholic Church of Southern Italy, the Macedonian Greek Catholic Church, the Romanian Church in union with Rome, the Greek-Catholic Church, the Russo-Greek Catholic Church; the Ruthenian Greek Catholic Church; the Slovak Greek Catholic Church and the Ukrainian Greek Catholic Church

Gynæconitis the name of the upper balcony on the interior of the Western Front of a great church where noble women were seated apart from the general population. The Eucharist was brought to these women as it was considered unseemly for them to mingle with the public. A separate stairwell led up to the balcony by way of a secluded entrance.

Habemus Papam the title of the solemn proclamation, meaning "We have a Pope" given from the central loggia of the Hall of Benedictions above the main entrance of Saint Peter's Basilica in the Vatican announcing to the world that a new pope has been elected in Sacred Conclave. The right to make this proclamation falls to the *protodeacon* of the Holy Roman Church assisted by the Papal Master of Ceremonies and those prelates attached to the ceremonial office at the Vatican, coming within the hour of a new pope's election and the first appearance of white smoke emanating from the chimney of the Sistine Chapel.

Annuntio vobis gaudium magnum
Habemus Papam
Eminentissimum ac reverendissimum Dominum,
Dominum [The New Pope's Actual First Name],
Sanctæ Romanæ Ecclesiæ Cardinalem [The New Pope's Actual Family Name],
Qui sibi nomen imposuit [The Name Chosen by the New Pope as his Reignal or Pontifical Name].

The English language translation reads: "I announce to you a great joy; We have a Pope! The Most Eminent and Most Reverend Lord (first name of the cardinal elected pope) Cardinal of the Holy Roman Church (the last name of the cardinal just elected) who takes to himself the name of (the name he has selected as his pontifical name)".

The first appearance of the new pope on the central loggia could take place immediately thereafter, as in the case of the election of Pope Benedict XVI, or could be delayed for a hour or so more depending upon the activity taking place within the conclave enclosure.

Harrowing of Hell the Old English phrase representing the triumph of Christ over death and the period of His decent into the land of the dead (Hell) between the moment of His death on the cross and His resurrection on Easter Sunday. The term is still used in some places in Britain to describe the hours between three o'clock in the afternoon on Good Friday and dawn on Easter Sunday morning.

hermit the title given to one who avoids society, removing himself from all, or most, contact with the civilized world for the purpose of seeking spiritual perfection. In some places, some hermits attached themselves to the charity of a church or religious house and were thus called *anchorites.* Both males and females could choose this form of spiritual existence.

Hero of the Christian Church a title used in the Anglican Church in place of 'Canonized Saint' for those persons after the break with Rome and the Reformation who would otherwise have been declared a saint of the Catholic Church under the same conditions prior to the schism with the papacy.

hierodeacon a monk in the Eastern traditions and the Orthodox Church who has simultaneously been permitted to be ordained a deacon in Holy Orders.

holy days of obligation in the USA, the church observes six holy days of obligation: these are – the Solemnity of Mary, Mother of God on 1 January; Ascension Thursday (which falls forty days after Easter each year); the Assumption of the Blessed Virgin Mary, 15th August; All Saints' Day, celebrated worldwide on 1 November; The Solemnity of the Immaculate Conception of the Blessed Virgin Mary on 8 December and Christmas Day. Some confusion arises when New Year's Day, the Assumption BVM, or All Saints' Day fall on a Saturday or Monday. Now on these days, the feast day is still observed on the liturgical calendar but the obligation to attend Mass is suspended. In past times when Europe was a Catholic continent, people worked a six day week. When work schedules in past centuries called for six day weeks, Catholics eagerly awaited holy days of obligation because they typically were given a day off from work. To accommodate these workers' need for rest, originally many more feasts were included in the holy day of obligation schedule. Each nations' bishops set the feasts to be observed and so not all nations observe the same holy days out of obligation to attend Mass.

holy oils one of the sacramentals of the church, blessed oil are used in the execution of the seven sacraments of the Catholic Church. Oil has long been considered sustenance of life, as is water, and thus came into the church in both a symbolic and liturgical way in the first century. There are several types of holy oils in the church used for the sacraments and for the blessings and consecrations of certain persons and things:

Oil of the Sick came into the church through the directive if the Apostle James who commanded his followers to anoint a sick man with oil as an intercession in the name of Jesus Christ. Formally known in Latin as, *Oleum Infirorum,* in the early church both the clergy and laity of high standing could perform the blessing of this oil. In time the blessing of the Oil of the Sick fell exclusively to the priests and between the third and eleventh centuries it was considered better to use oil blessed simultaneously by seven priests gather together for this purpose. It is today used by the priest and bishop for the Sacrament of the Sick and is likewise used to bless (baptize) new bells to be used in the spires of churches. This oil contains a bit of wine and ashes in the mixture.

Oil of Catechumens came into use in the church in last half of the second century and in addition to being used for the blessing of those soon to be received into the church at Easter, it was also used in the ordination of priests and for the anointing rites of the Holy Roman Emperor (beginning with Charlemagne in AD 800) and all Catholic kings and queens thereafter. It is known in the Latin as *Oleum Sanctum* because this is a pure oil blessed by the bishop and is used in the rite of baptism and for the consecration rites of new churches.

Oils of Chrism reserved for the sacrament of Confirmation as the matter of that sacrament, came into general use in the church in the early fifth century. It is also used in baptism, and when a newly ordained priest so desires, it is used to bless his chalice and other sacred vessels. Known in Latin as *Sanctum Chrisma,* taking its name from the scent of ointment that this oil creates. This thickness and texture comes from a small amount of balsam (a resin taken from the terebinth tree) that is mixed with the oil in the blessing rite on Holy Thursday in every cathedral of the Catholic world.

Note: Those oils left over at the conclusion of the liturgical year are not to be retained or mixed with new oils. Rather, the church mandates that they be burned.

Oils for the Agnus Dei are not sacramentals of the church but were used s such for the creation of the papal award of the Agnus Dei medallion. This award was made of a mixture of wax and blessed oil, which had to be collected on Holy Thursday from the Archpriest and Archdeacon of the Papal Basilica of Saint John Lateran. (See: *Agnus Dei)*

Holy Orders, fullness of there are three classes, or ranks within Holy Orders Deacon, Priest and Bishop. There are two types of deaconate, the permanent deaconate for men who never intend to go forward to priestly ordination (open to married men) and the transitional deaconate, those who await the call to priesthood but who have entered into orders in the office of deacon.

Priesthood is the second rank in Holy Orders and the office that the great majority of clerics attain. Only a small segment of the clergy are ever called to the Office of Bishop, known also as the Episcopal dignity. When this happens, it is said that this cleric has attained the *fullness of Holy Orders,* that is to say, he has attained all three offices within this sacrament.

Holy Week the seven days leading into the liturgical celebration of Easter commemorating the Betrayal, Judgment, Passion, Crucifixion, and

Death of Jesus Christ but theologically considered to be inseparable from the Easter miracle that follows. Although historically each day of Holy Week marked a special scriptural event, the modern liturgy fixes Holy Thursday and Good Friday as the main days of commemoration of the Passion of Christ. Holy Week is also considered to be the end of the forty daylong Lenten period of preparation It formally opens at Palm Sunday and closes before the Easter Vigil on Holy Saturday evening.

hours, canonical the term applied to the fixed times at which the various segments of the Liturgy of the Hours are to be recited.

Hours, Liturgy of the once known as the Divine Office

hyperdulia the proper Latin term for the act of veneration of the Blessed Virgin Mary.

ICHTHYS the Greek word for 'fish' and the original symbol of the early Christians. Before the Cross of Calvary was adopted in the mid-third century as the universal symbol for Christianity, the small underground persecuted community of Christ's earliest followers used the symbol of the fish, painted on their door portals and other personal property, so that other believers could find a safe house and a place where the Sacrifice of the Last Supper could be celebrated in common. The choice of the symbol of the fish came to the early church from the miracle of the loafs and fishes.

Immediately Subject to the Holy See the canonical term that defines ecclesiastical territories such as archdioceses, dioceses, archeparchies, eparchies, any abbey nullius and all other similar jurisdictions that report to the Holy See with no other canonical authority above them. Examples of some of these would be: the Archdioceses of Liechtenstein, Luxembourg and Monaco and the territorial abbeys of Santa Maria in Einsiedeln and Saint Maurice (both in Switzerland) and Montecassino (in Italy).

Imprimatur the formal grant of ecclesiastical approval by the local bishop designating a theological work to be published as being in conformity with the formal teaching of the Catholic Church. Under Canon

Law, only theological and/or liturgical works require the formal consent of the Church. Church histories, Catholic biographies, and non-dogmatic works are exempt from the mandate of the formal grant of the *imprimatur*.

incardination the canonical term meaning to belong to one diocese in the same sense that one spouse belongs to another. Deacons, priests and bishops are incardinated to their diocese. For a cleric to leave one diocese for another, in the permanent sense, one must be *excardinated,* meaning to formally leave in good standing with the church's blessing. The process is quite lengthy but not particularly difficult to achieve.

incense a symbolic sacramental of the Church, which came to us from ancient Jewish tradition like so many of our customs and practices. It is mentioned in the book of Exodus, throughout the Psalms, and by the prophets Jeremiah and Isaiah. As such, it was an integral part of early Jewish worship and from the earliest days of the Christian Church it enjoyed an honored position in liturgical life. It is mentioned in the Nativity narratives of Sacred Scripture, citing it as one of the gifts of the Magi to the Christ-child under its formal name – *frankincense* (the gift of *myrrh* is also a resin from which incense is derived).

Incense, like amber, is a resin that is harvested from the terebinth genus of trees found throughout the Middle East and other sub-tropical countries. When dried and rendered into aromatic powders, incense burns freely on hot coals emitting a powerful fragrance and colorful smoke that enhances sacred worship. It is called the "symbolic sacramental" because by its very nature, it calls to mind the role of common prayer 'that rises like smoke up to Heaven as a petition from the children of God'. The use of incense in Catholic worship has always been reserved for the most important liturgical celebrations. It has held additional significance for Eastern Catholics where this aromatic resin has played a far more vital role in all aspects of liturgical life in the Oriental rites of the Church.

In the past, celebrations making use of incense were referred to as Solemn High Masses. Today, liturgies presided over by the pope, cardinals, bishops, and by priests on important feast days are informally prescribed as incense Masses. The fragrance is expelled from a silver or golden orb-like container known as a *censor* or *thurible* that is suspended on chains that allow for a functionary of the liturgy (known as a *thurifer)* to swing it liberally which aids in the escape of both smoke and fragrance.

Although incense is present throughout the entirety of these special liturgies, it is most effectively used to reverence the Crucifix, to honor the Book of the Gospels, at the preparation of the gifts and the altar of sacrifice, and at the elevation of both species of the Blessed Sacrament. Special prayers have long been proscribed for each particular incensation, which the celebrant recites in silence. Incense is also used by the Church to venerate the deceased at the close of the funeral rites for baptized Catholics.

In Commendam an appointment in the Church, rarely seen today, in which a prelate (typically an archbishop, bishop, or abbot) was given numerous posts at the same time. This was the custom at a time when those who were elevated to these high offices were themselves of high birth. The title refers to the trust the church places in one person to govern or to possess.

The reason for these *in Commendam* appointments was that all the *benefices*, or financial gain, that were attached to each appointment was given to the prelate who held all of these offices simultaneously, thus enriching him beyond imagination. An accumulation of these many Church titles were also much sought after that that time. A *legate, or vicar* would then be sent in this highborn churchmen's place to govern the place. Today, only honorary *in-Commendam* appointments are permitted and for the past one hundred years, the popes have only granted 'in commendam' appointments to the cardinals resident in Rome.

indulgence a term that literally translates from the Latin, *indulgentia,* meaning "to extend kindness in one's mercy" and which the church uses to describe the act of "remission from the temporal punishment due to sin, the quilt from which has been forgiven and the faithful Christian, who is duly disposed, gains under certain prescribed conditions through the action of the church, which as minister of redemption, dispenses and applies with authority the satisfaction of Christ and the Saints" (n. 1471,

Catechism of the Catholic Church). Indulgences may be applied to both the living and the souls in Purgatory and may be partial or plenary (full) dependent upon the grant issued in each application.

indult an indult, or papal indult, is a special privilege or faculty granted to bishops or priests by the Holy See to do something other than the norm, such as permission to eat meat on Friday during Lent, however, it is typically applied to more serious actions.

in odium fidei a Latin phrase attached to the state of grace at the moment of death, especially the death of a martyr, which translates literally to '*in the odor of the faith*' but which more generally has come to be understood as 'being in pure sanctity' and which refers to the deceased being in a perfect state of grace at the moment that he or she was killed for the faith.

in partibus infidelium the Latin phrase meaning 'in the lands of the non-believers' which is attached to the end of the title of all titular bishops who have been assigned a titular see in a place where Islam took control of the church after the sixth century. It is the only place in the church where the use of the word 'infidel' is found.

in persona episcopi the Latin phrase meaning 'in the person of the bishop' which is applied to the rare instance when a bishop of one diocese is given permanent governance of another without relinquishing the first so that he enjoys the full powers, rights, and the same canonical standing of any other appointed bishop of a diocese in both Sees, thereafter permanently governing both dioceses simultaneously.

in poenam the Latin phrase applied under canon law to the imposition of ecclesial penalties. This translates in English to "as a form of penalty" and is applied to specific actions taken by Rome where error exists. Most recently Pope Benedict XVI extended the faculties or competence of the Congregation of the Clergy in Rome to extend censure and remedy to priests who may have attempted to marry outside of their priestly vows or to priests who do not exercise priestly ministries for extended periods other than for reasons of health. Legal actions taken against these clerics were imposed "in poenam."

institutes, pontifical those religious or secular institutes of men or women that are formally recognized by the Holy See.

institutes, religious those societies of Consecrated or Apostolic Life that have been awarded formal recognition by the local bishop or by the Holy See. The members, male or female, live in common and profess public vows but these may be either perpetual (permanent) or temporary.

institutes, secular erected as a modern form of vocation by Pope Pius XII in 1948, these societies must have a unique charism, or mission, and form their members along more secular lines in society. Whereas religious institutes model themselves after the old orders, the secular institutes do not. For instance, most members of the secular institutes even provide for their own health insurance and other financial needs.

interdict the formal prohibition or censure by church authorities on a person or a group of people, such as an entire nation, from participating in the sacraments of the church. Such a grave step is rarely promulgated and only in grave sinfulness. The interdict is so serious and act, that if a person, area, or nation (as in the case of England in 1215) is placed under interdict the faithful prohibited may not even receive a Christian burial at the time of death.

internal forum the theological term, protected under the codes of Canon Law, referring to those discussions with a priest or bishop undertaken under the "seal of the confessional". Internal forum discussions include a sacramental confession made by a penitent as well as those rare occasions when private matters are specifically entrusted to a priest or bishop with the understanding that the topic of discussion, although no confession of sin is made, must be protected in the same manner as discussions within the Sacrament of Penance.

international shrine a title assigned to a formally erected shrine of the church, which because of its unique character is either the sole example of this particular devotion and/or spirituality or is the foundation of a huge international movement. An example of an international shrine would be the Basilica of Divine Mercy in Krakow, Poland. International shrines may simultaneously be cathedrals, basilicas, parish churches or abbey churches.

irremovability the ecclesiastical principle that an office holder in the church enjoys his office for life. Today only a pope holds an irremovable office. All other senior prelates may be removed at the will of the pope and must also resign from office at age seventy-five. But before Vatican II, and the changes that followed, most offices of governance in the church were considered irremovable. Even pastors and rectors more or less could not be removed, except for grave cause.

Italo-Greek Rite also known as the Albanesese Rite. See: *Rites of the Church*

J

jurisdictions (of the Latin Rite) the types of jurisdictions within the Latin Rite include the following titles in descending rank: the Petrine Office (papacy), patriarchal sees (residential and titular), major archiepiscopal sees, metropolitan archiepiscopal sees (residential and titular), archiepiscopal sees (residential and titular), episcopal sees (residential and titular), vicariates apostolic (residential and titular), prefectures apostolic, abbacies nullius (territorial), abbacies, titular abbacies, prelatures nullius (territorial), personal prelatures (residential and titular), military ordinariates, apostolic prefectures, administrations apostolic, personal administrations apostolic, and missions 'sui iuris'.

jus exclusivae the canonical Latin phrase meaning *royal veto*; the right of certain Catholic monarchs before 1903 to impose a veto against a specific candidate for the papacy during the conclave electing a pope because of a personal or state distaste for a specific cardinal candidate. Those claiming this right at various times in history were the Holy Roman Emperors, the Emperors of Austria and the kings of France and Spain and Bavaria amongst others. When it was imposed, the monarch's veto was imposed by the *crown-cardinal* of that realm that had been mandated by the monarch to deny a specific cardinal the papacy.

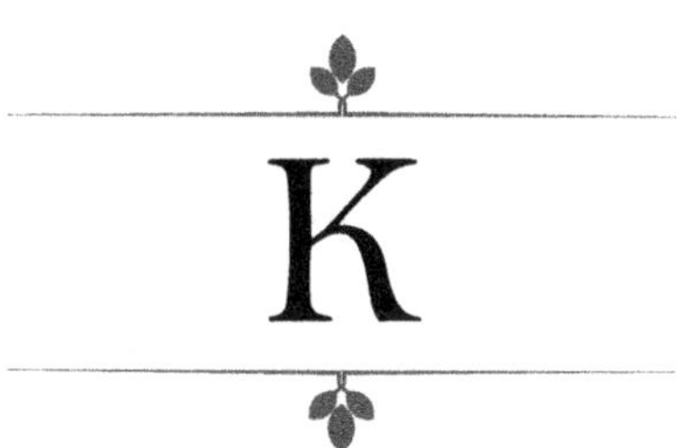

kissing the palms the deferential and respectful gesture in which bishops, priests, and the faithful kiss the consecrated palms of a newly ordained priest. This custom, reverencing both the sacrament of Holy Orders and the Chrism used in the sacrament dates to the second century.

Kyrie Eleison from the Greek meaning "Lord Have Mercy," the only part of the Mass sequences that come into the liturgy of the Latin Rite in Greek. This sequence came into the Church of Rome from the East in the second century. It their entireties there are three supplications forming this sequence: Lord Have Mercy (which is a plea in honor of God the Father), Christ Have Mercy (which is a plea directed to Jesus, the Son of God), and Lord Have Mercy (which is a plea in honor of God the Holy Spirit). In the old liturgy, this sequence was repeated three times for each supplication. The modern liturgy has retained the Greek formula while at the same time embracing the vernacular and the chant mode used varies from Gregorian plainchant to African tribal folk music.

Laetare the fourth Sunday in Lent corresponding to Gaudate Sunday in Advent. One of the two Rose Sundays, so called as the purple vestments of the season are replaced with the less somber rose, or pink, color. The term comes from the Latin Indroit of the Mass, *Laetare Jerusalem,* which translates to 'Rejoice, oh Jerusalem.' It falls just after the middle of Lent (the Thursday prior to Laetare Sunday is the actual mid-point of the penitential season) and was inserted into the Lenten Season in the seventh century.

lantern the open space at the top of a dome so that light can enter the church below. The "lantern" atop the dome of St. Peter's Basilica, for instance, is worked in a series of sixteen dual decorative columns surrounding it, in between each is found a window as a source of light for the church far below.

Lateran the seat of the Bishop of Rome and the home of the papacy from the first century through to the Avignon Exile of the thirteenth century and thereafter again until the move to the Quirinale Palace in the sixteenth century. After the popes settled at the Quirinale, the Lateran never again served as the seat of the papacy but throughout the entire history of the Roman episcopacy, the Lateran has served as its seat. It is here in this complex that is found the Lateran Basilica of Saint John, the actual cathedral of Rome and thus the pope's (in his capacity as Bishop of Rome) church. Here also is a massive palace that was first begun in the third century and which was greatly expanded upon throughout the centuries. This palace was the host of the treaty negotiations between the Italian State and the Holy See in 1929 which ended the Roman Question and which founded the new Vatican City State. It is also the home of the pope's Vicar for Rome. This complex is the site of the prestigious Pontifical Lateran University, one of the finest in Europe.

Lateran Basilica officially the 'Archbasilica of the Most Holy Savior and Saint John the Baptist and Evangelist in the Lateran' and the official cathedral church of Rome. The Lateran Basilica is considered to be the Mother Church of Christianity and its title is rendered in Latin as the *Archbasilica di Santissimo Salvatore e Sante Giovanni Battista ed Evangelista al Laterano.* The cathedral-basilica of Rome, the Lateran is dedicated to Jesus Christ but has as its sub-dedication Saint John the Baptist. Unique to this church, there is also a tertiary dedication, to Saint John the Evangelist, sometimes also known as 'the Divine.' It is this church that is the main church of the bishop of Rome although the pope celebrates many more liturgies at the Vatican Basilica of Saint Peter.

Lateran Museum the collection officially entitled the Profane Museum of the Lateran Palace, founded by Pope Pius IX in 1854 to house the secular exhibits of the Papal Court and the institution of the papacy. It was merged with the collection founded by Pope Gregory XVI, which was founded in 1843, and which included exhibits of the early Christian period. Today the Lateran Museum is administered by the Papal Vicariate for Rome and is typically opened every other Sunday afternoon.

Lateran Treaties the diplomatic pacts of 1929 between the Italian kingdom and the Holy See, engineered in part by Benito Mussolini and Cardinal Secretary of State Gaspar, which ended the self-embossed exile of the popes within the walls of the Vatican Apostolic Palace after the fall of Rome to the *Risorgimento.* Out of these treaties came the creation of the smallest nation-state in Europe, the 100-acre Vatican City State. The Italian government offered more land to the church but Pope Pius XI refused saying that he needed only enough land to be recognized as a sovereign and thus guarantee international independence. The treaties also returned other properties throughout the city and the region around Rome, designating them as extra-territorial (that is to say not subject to the law of Italy and subject only to the popes) and made retribution payments for all the other territories, buildings, and investments of the church lost after 1870. The Lateran Treaties were of two natures: nation to nation and nation to church. As such, these pacts also include a separate document, the Concordat, which is a diplomatically worded treaty between the Church and a nation-state. This church-state document recognized the Roman Catholic faith as the official religion of the Italian nation and offered special prerogatives to the Catholic Church within Italy.

Latin cross a cross form where the vertical arm is longer than the horizontal arm. Again, St. Peter's Basilica is an ideal form of this cross-type church, thanks in large measure to Pope Paul V and Maderno who made extensive changes to Michelangelo's original design, which originally called for a Greek Cross design.

latria the proper Latin term for the act of worship, in itself much more substantive than an act of veneration accorded to the Blessed Virgin Mary or to the saints, for the Three Persons of God.

laudatio the special tribute read aloud in a public setting, such at a consistory, convocation or commencement ceremony, praising the gifts and talents of the one present being honored.

lavabo the liturgical ritual within the Mass at which the celebrant washes his fingers. This custom came into the Mass in 1570 with the Roman revisions to the Missal that year but its origins are quite ancient, reaching back into the Old Testament. Psalm 25 reads in the Latin Vulgate: "Lavabo inter innocents manus meas" which translates to I will wash my hands amongst the innocents. It is from this formula that the ritual took its name.

lay religious the place in the hierarchy of the church after the deacon and the religious (who are also priests and deacons) but before the general laity. Most people do not realize that nearly all the communities of sisters established after 1800 are communities of persons amongst the laity, living in consecrated life and are not amongst the classes of the clergy (naturally) or the religious. Such orders are the Religious Sister of Mercy, the Sister of Saint Joseph, the Sister of Notre Dame, the Sisters of Charity and many, many more. These women are called 'Sisters' rather than nuns, which they technically are not although they did dress as such from the outset of their foundations. The male equivalent would be the lay brother, one who will never be ordained a priest such as the Brother of Christian Schools.

Lectionary the title for the book containing all of the readings for the Mass and the exercise of the Sacraments and which is typically carried in procession at the opening of the Liturgy of the Eucharist. It is divided into cycles mandated by the Church so that the readings for each Sunday liturgy vary from year to year within the proscribed cycle.

Legation a diplomatic term used to describe a mission not accorded the rank of embassy, or in other words a mission headed by a full ambassador. After the Second World War, the United States government no longer sent Legations abroad nor would they permit a nation to accredit any mission less than a full embassy. The Holy See used this term in the same manner up to the same historic period but no longer makes use of it. If the Holy Father's representative is not accredited as a full ambassador (under the term *nuncio* but rather only as a representative to the Church (not to the Church and the government of a given country) he is known as *Apostolic Delegate* and his mission is called an *Apostolic Delegation*. The papacy maintained another form of the term *Legation* for many centuries; as the title for the governments set up by the popes to govern the regions of Ferrara, Bologna, and Romagna when the Papal States were at their zenith.

Lexio Divino a term meaning the Word of God and pertaining to the Divine Office.

licentiate the level of academic degree found beneath that of the doctorate in pontifical universities. In comparison to other levels of degrees, the licentiate ranks above a master's degree but below the doctorate.

liturgy from the Greek '*leitourgia' meaning a solemn act of public service or good will traditionally undertaken by the wealthy in aid of the poor. When it came into use in the early church (first century), it came to mean the solemn acts and rituals performed by the priests and bishops for the people in the same way the wealthy would perform sincere acts of goodwill for the poor. The term soon came to take on two distinct meanings as the Catholic Church developed— as applied to the group of total rites, ceremonies, rituals, sacramentals and prayers of the church performed in public and also as it is specifically applied to the Holy Sacrifice of the Mass which in the post Vatican II era has been most often called 'the liturgy' or 'the sacred liturgy.'*

Lord's Prayer the English language title for the *Pater noster,* known also as the 'Our Father'. Recited only in Latin until the post-Reformation period, the title 'Lord's Prayer' is actually more Anglican than it is Roman, although it is found in the lexicon of both churches. The words are Christ's own found in both the Gospel of Saint Matthew and Saint Luke and have been accurately translated from the Vulgate. The Protestants, through an insertion into the Anglican 'Book of Common Prayer', added the doxology, 'for Thine is the Kingdom…" which they had taken from an appearance in later Greek translations of the original Gospel citation, but which was not found the original.

The Pater Noster was the one prayer that rich and poor alike shared in the first centuries of the church. Because serving brothers in the monasteries of the Middle Ages did not master Latin until after several years in residence, they could not join in on the choral recitation of the Divine Office. Instead, these young clerics recited a series of Pater Nosters in silence during the general singing of the Divine Office. To help in this task, a rope chain was created with ten little knots worked into it. Each knot represented one Pater Noster. This mode of prayer predated the design of the Holy Rosary.

Liber Pontificalis the earliest history of the papacy, in the form of biographical treatises, beginning with Saint Peter and continuing into the fifteenth century. Although the information contained within these texts is generally believed to be accurate there are no proves available to verify the earliest histories, especially those from Saint Peter to Pope Stephen V (AD 885-891). As such, the church does not hold the early histories up as completely authentic. Several different, unknown authors penned the *Liber Pontificalis.* The source material for most of these is beyond reproach, thus the church's embrace of most of the studies.

litany a form of liturgical prayer of the church. From the Latin, *litania,* meaning prayerful supplication; a prayer originally developed to implore God to come to the aid of His people in need. The typical litany is composed as a repeating formula, after each individual supplication the formula ends in '*hear our prayer*', or '*hear us O Lord*'. The most famous litanies in the church are: *The Litany of the Saints, The Litany of Loretto,* and *The Litany to the Sacred Heart* and *The Litany of Saint Joseph* and *The Litany of the Holy Name of Jesus.*

liturgy a term from the Greek, *leitourgia,* meaning to undertake a public service or duty; the rite of the Holy Sacrifice of the Mass. Technically this term encompasses all of the many public rites, ceremonies, sacraments and prayers of both the Roman and the Greek churches. Although this is so, in the Roman church, it is most commonly applied to the celebration of the Eucharist.

liturgists those persons appointed by the diocesan bishop to protect the rituals and ceremonies of the liturgy and sacraments of the church, the liturgical life of the diocese, and to direct the episcopal ceremonies of the bishop(s). These persons are typically priests but may be deacons, religious or lay members of the faithful that must possess both a full understanding of the liturgical rubrics, historical ceremonial, and rituals of the Holy Roman Church as well as the ability to faithfully adhere to Roman mandate. One of the foremost roles of a diocesan bishop in the post-conciliar age is to assure the appointment of both a capable and faithful diocesan liturgist within his territory so as to avoid serious scandal and ritual error.

loggia a large arcade on the second or third floor of a palatial building. Also a term applied to a quiet corridor within a monastery, abbey or seminary.

lying in repose the term applied within the church and in civil protocol describing the period of time after the death of a dignitary who is neither a pope or head of state when the earthly remains are placed on public display before burial. In the Church, cardinals, patriarchs, archbishops and bishops 'lie in repose' in a church of their jurisdiction as do pastors within their parishes. In civil protocol non-heads of state of all ranks, such as royal family members, prime ministers, governors and governors-general et al all 'lie in repose' in the place of their authority. It is never said of these personages that they 'lie in state.'

lying in state the term applied to the period of time after the death of a pope or head of state when the body is publicly viewed. The difference between the status of 'lying in state' and 'lying in repose' is that heads of state receive an honor guard of military or high pontifical rank at all times during this period and for the days when the body is placed on public view this site becomes the focus of an entire nation, or in the case of a deceased pope, the entire Church. Great ceremonial is attached to the period of 'lying in state' which can last from anywhere from three to six days before burial and is always orchestrated in a grand public facility. During this time the earthly remains are never left alone, even if public viewing has ended for the day. Most often, in terms of both deceased popes and heads of state, a private viewing period for family members and close associates precedes the official 'lying in state'. This event could correctly be referred to as either the *Rite of Viewing* and/or a 'lying in repose'.

mace a staff of wood or metal with an elaborate, global top, which is highly ornamented and used exclusively for processions. Until 1969, the bearer of the mace was one of the official positions of the Papal Court.

Magi sometimes also referred to as the "Three Kings", the "Three Wise Men", and also as the "Three Astronomers", the first prominent visitors to the Holy Family after the birth of the Christ-child, drawn to the Holy Land by the Star of Bethlehem. It is not certain how much time passed before the *Magi* arrived at Bethlehem but their homage alerted King Herod of the fulfillment of the ancient prophecy announcing the coming of the Messiah, or Savior, of the Jewish people.

Although it is certainly only pious legend, through the ages the names of the *Magi* have been given as *Gaspar*, *Balthazar*, and *Melchior*. Ancient tales described the Magi for the early Christians' veneration: The first of these was Melchior. Legend tells us that Melchior was the high king of Arabia and India at the time of Christ's birth. This area is known today as Mesopotamia in Iraq. He was said to be small in stature, kindly but very elderly, a man renowned for his piety. Melchior was the oldest of the three magi who followed the star to Bethlehem. As such, his figurine is always placed the closest to the crèche and the Christ Child out of deference to age and power.

Artists long have depicted Melchior as a very ancient prince with a long, white beard. He is always vested in purple or scarlet, the colors of royalty at that time in history. Tradition tells us that Melchior was very cultured and wise and enjoyed the lute and harp more than any other instrument. It is believed that he kept musicians in his caravans who played these instruments unceasingly and that this music was the first heard by the Christ Child once the magi arrived at Bethlehem.

Melchior, it is said, waited many decades for the star of Bethlehem to appear so that he could finally begin his long awaited pilgrimage to find the promised Messiah. When he set out, Melchior carried a gold casket filled with rare gold coins with him to present to the Christ Child. Scholars also note that he carried rare silks and precious stones and one historian of the early church wrote that King Melchior literally rolled out these treasures before the crib of the infant and at the feet of Mary and Joseph in an array of brilliant color and sparkling gems. Pious legend tells us that Melchior lived until one hundred sixteen years, his age when he finally arrived at Bethlehem. It was on the eight day after his arrival at the home of the Holy Family, while praying at the Temple, that he collapse and died, his lifelong pilgrimage completed. As was the custom, the other two kings, Gaspar and Balthazar, were with Melchior in the Temple and it was they who led his procession to burial.

If Melchior was the oldest of the Wise Men than Gaspar was known to be the youngest but not by much as it is said that he died in the same year at age one hundred nine years. Gaspar was the King of Tharsis and was said to be the richest king on earth at that time, far more wealthy in fact than the Roman emperor. Like Melchior, Gaspar was known for his love of music but his was an interest in traditional tribal lullabies if his youth. True to his ethnic origins, Gaspar is always depicted wearing a richly embroidered silk turban. His gift to the Christ Child was frankincense laced with gold dust. It is also said that he carried a gold casket of polished diamonds which he spread across the clothe previously laid down by Melchior. Incense, as frankincense is now know, is aromatic and comes in a variety of rich 'flavors' each emanating a different fragrance. Then, as now, the sweet smoke of incense represented the prayers and hopes of the faithful reaching upward into Heaven and so it is believed that upon his arrival at the crèche, while Melchior's harp and lute played the sweet smell of burning incense also filled the humble abode. Gaspar is always depicted at the crèche standing slightly distant from Melchior, a sign of respect to the senior king, allowing Melchior to prostrate himself to the Infant Jesus before all others.

Balthazar, the last of the three magi, travelled the farthest. It is said of him that he arrived with his clothes worn and tattered although after meeting Herod to seek out the Messiah's whereabouts, he changed into regal finery to meet the Christ Child. Balthazar was an African king, most probably the King of Saba. As such he is historically referred to as an Ethiopian *magus* or *negus* (king). It is believed that he arrived by elephant in a caravan of more than 300 beasts of that species, the first time this beast was seen in the Holy Land. His gift to the Infant Jesus was myrrh. Myrrh is a valuable resin that is collected from the bark of thorny African trees, although this species is also found in southern Arabia near present day Oman. The resin was treasured across the Holy Land at the time of Christ's birth because it was known to stop insects and rodents from infesting a house when the dried plant was pressed into a form of incense; the strong aroma was offensive to vermin. Scripture scholars link Myrrh to suffering and as such they infer that Balthazar was foretelling what was to come to the Messiah on Calvary.

Pious legend has it that when Balthazar arrived at the crèche, his balky urn carrying the gift of Myrrh awoke the Christ Child who it was said smiled sweetly upon his face. It has been said that Balthazar lived to the age of one hundred twelve, dying one year after both Melchior and Gaspar.

The three titles for the historic visitors to the Christ Child have specific purpose in identifying Jesus as Son of God. The title of *Magi* is an ancient one that translates to 'astromener'; they are the people who were the most educated in the ancient world and the ones that best understood the science of the heavens and so the identification of these visitors as *Magi* signifies that even the most brilliant of mankind recognized Jesus as Son of God. The title of *Wise Men* complements this concept in that the wisest of mankind, the greatest thinkers and philosophers, came to know the Child Jesus as God. It is important to note that the Wise Men are said to come out of the east because in the ancient world the belief was that wisdom was found 'in the east' and that the wisest of men came from there. The third common title, *Three Kings,* represents the great leaders of the world and how even great rulers came to subjugate themselves to the Child Savior. This is important in fulfillment of the Old Testament in which it was written in Psalm 72 about the coming of the Savior: *The kings of Tarshish and the Isles shall offer gifts; the kings of Arabia and Seba shall bring tribute. All kings shall pay him homage, all nations shall serve him.* This text not only foretells the arrival of the Magi but also is symbolic of the subjugation of all peoples great and small to the Son of God.

Magisterium the term applied to the legal teaching authority of the hierarchy of the Roman Catholic Church. The term comes from the Latin, *magister,* meaning teacher. The pope and the College of Bishops together form the official Magisterium of the Church.

Malabar Rite See: *Rites of the Church*

manaturgium a elaborately embroidered white linen cloth used by a newly ordained priest to cleanse his hands after the sacred *chrism* of ordination has been applied. This cleansing ritual also includes lemons, water and salt to ceremoniously remove the oils in a respectful manner. The *Manaturgium* is then used to wipe clean the residue. This cloth is then reserved for the future and is placed in the casket of the priest's mother as a reminder that she gave a son to the Church.

maniple a seldom seen vestment resembling a scarf or napkin that priests wore with Roman style vestments over the forearm. Also known as the mappa and the *mappula,* this garment came into the church as a vestment as early as the first century. Before this time it was worn on the toga of the most wealthy and powerful Roman citizens as a form of decoration. When it came into the church, it was used exclusively at the Communion Rite for the protection of the Precious Blood. Until the fourth century, it had been optional. Then in AD 330 Pope Sylvester mandated for use throughout the Roman Province. By the seventh century it was granted to the deacon and sub-deacon (now abolished). In the tenth century jewels and rich cloth were exchanged for the simple white linen napkin that it had been from the outset. Until it was laid aside after Vatican II, the maniple resembled the vestment worn in both color and material no longer able to be used by priests to wipe the face and hands. The maniple is rarely seen today and when it is, it is used only with the more elaborate Roman-style vestments.

manteau, altar railing a fine linen clothe the length of a fixed altar railing often decorated with lace, used mainly in Spain and Portugal as a means to protect the Blessed Sacrament from reaching the floor were it to fall from the priest's hand at the Communion Rite. Typically, the kneeling communicants pull this manteau up to the chest to assure that were the Eucharist to fall it would come to rest on clean clothe. In the United States, an example of the *altar railing manteau* may be found at the Shrine of the Blessed Sacrament at the Monastery of Our Lady of the Angels in Hanceville in Alabama.

mardi gras from the French for 'Fat Tuesday', the day before Ash Wednesday when Lent officially begins. A day of great celebration and feasting, also known as *Carnivale.* An approved day of libation before the severity of the Lenten sacrifice began.

martyrium a church or cathedral built over a known tomb of a saint of the church, in particular, one martyred for the faith. The two most famous of these shrines are found in Rome: The Vatican Basilica of Saint Peter (built over the known tomb of the Prince of the Apostles) and the Papal Basilica of Saint Paul Outside-the-Walls (over the tomb of Saint Paul).

Martyrologium Romanum the church's formal catalog of all the known martyrs and saints assigning to each a feast day on the liturgical calendar.

Mass, the the liturgy of the church which takes its name from the word for *meal.*

Mass, capitular the Mass that is celebrated inside a cathedral where a chapter of canons presides or in a collegiate church where canons reside. The title derives from the word "chapter" meaning college of canons. The capitular Mass is usually a High Mass at which all of the canons of the place take part in full vesture of their office. Perhaps the most famous of these today is the capitular Mass celebrated each Sunday in Saint Peter's Basilica in which the canons process from their chapter chapel through the basilica in purple vesture.

Mass cards the title for the gift of 'in memoriam' Masses or Masses to be celebrated for the sick or for the well being of another. Typically, a religious order, parish, or other proper ecclesial authority supplies a formal document or religious greeting card that permits the gift giver to list the Masses to be celebrated and under what circumstances it shall be celebrated. In turn, the ecclesial authority accepts the stipend to celebrate the Mass and then does so in accordance with the terms of the document created. Typically, the gift of an 'in memoriam' Mass card is the most common Catholic form of condolence at the time of death of a loved one. Note to be confused with 'Altar cards" which were the cards displayed on the altar and which were used in the old liturgy displaying the rituals for celebrating the Mass

Mass, conventual the Mass that is generally celebrated inside cloistered convents, monasteries and priories. The Order of Saint John of Jerusalem, of Rhoades, and of Malta (known as the Knights of Malta) refer to their institutions as 'convents' in some instances and Masses celebrated in these places are also known properly as conventual Masses.

Mass, high a term seldom used today to define the celebration of a Sunday or funeral Mass that is almost entirely sung or chanted and where a deacon is also present. Today, little designation is made in the form of the celebration of a Mass by the lower clergy.

Mass, low the term used at one time to describe a Mass with no music of any kind.

Mass, papal the term used to describe a Mass at which the pope, himself, is the principal celebrant.

Mass, parochial the term applied by the church to refer simply to the Sunday Mass or Mass on Holy Days of Obligation and those on high feasts celebrated within the parish for the parish.

Mass, pontifical the term used by the church to describe a High Mass celebrated by the local bishop. One would think that a pontifical Mass would be that celebrated by the pope but this is not the case as the term 'pontifical' in this instance refers to the vesture and vestments worn by bishops on special occasions and which are known properly as 'pontificals'.

Mass, requiem the term once used by the church to describe the funeral liturgy. It took its name from the opening words of the old Latin Mass, which read: "Requiem aeternam dona eis, Domine" and which translates into English as "Eternal Rest grant unto them, O Lord ."

Mass, solemn the term for the most formal Mass that a priest could celebrate by himself. It required elaborate music, the presence of a deacon, and the use of incense at appropriate times. Today, no such designation formally exists as each priest may celebrate the liturgy as he sees fit for any given occasion.

Mass, votive from the Latin, *votum,* or vow this Mass is one celebrated out of the sequence of the normal liturgical seasons at the intent of the celebrating priest.

master of ceremonies in secular times the person charged with organizing public ceremonies. In ecclesial terms, the Master of Ceremonies is responsible for the smooth exercise of the Sacred Liturgy. A diocesan bishop typically appoints one priest as his permanent Master of Ceremonies and he not only accompanies the bishop throughout the diocese but also must make certain that the liturgical and sacramental life of the diocese is in conformity with church regulations.

medals, devotional a sacramental of the church used to foster an increase in devotion. Also known as religious medals, this sacramental came into the church from the ancient Roman Empire that routinely used money or coin size metal worked with effigies of important members of Roman society as a way to honor victors in combat. These medallions were worn around the neck outside of the clothing for all to readily admire. The Christians created their own versions of these tributes as early as the first half of the second century, mainly in honor of the early martyrs, but because of persecution, they wore them secretly beneath the clothing (and from this custom the practice continues today of wearing medals under clothing).

Later the church formalized this devotion, coining images of the Lord and properly recognized saints for use with clerical dress. By the eighth century the laity also adopted this custom and by the twelve century nearly every saint had a medallion coined in their honor. The most famous medals were those used in difficult times, such as times of plaque or war. The Medal of Saint Benedict was considered to be powerful in the intercession against the plaque known commonly as the *Black Death.* Other medals developed in time, the most famous of these being, the Miraculous Medal (known officially as the medal of the Blessed Virgin Mary of the Immaculate Conception) and worn throughout the world by millions of Catholics. The French church created it after the visionary, Saint Catherine Labouré, recalled the design she had been given for it by the Blessed Virgin at her Parisian convent on the rue de Bac.

Melkites, Greek A member church of the Byzantine Rite of the Catholic Church

Memoriale Rituum or the Memorial of Rites, a liturgical text that was used for the consecrations and blessings of the church, in particular for sacramentals.

military ordinate the diocese erected as a personal jurisdiction serving the diplomats and the armed forces of a nation wherever they may be stationed in the world. The head of a military ordinate is usually an archbishop.

Minims the name of a religious order of mendicant friars founded by Saint Francis de Paolo with roots in the Franciscan movement. Its name was taken from the Vulgate referring to the members as being 'the humblest of the humble' which transfers to be the most minimal of the servants of God. The order flourished in Italy, France, Spain, Latin America as well as in Germany and Austria but it never took root in English speaking countries.

Minster the Old English title for a cathedral, such as *York Minster* meaning the cathedral of York in northern England. Although this was the term for cathedrals prior to the Reformation, the title of 'Minster' is generally only now applied to Anglican cathedrals, including those that were originally Roman Catholic.

Missal, Roman the term used for the Altar book or the book used for the celebration of the Mass. It is also the term used for an abbreviated version of the same used by the faithful to follow the Mass. This term is rarely used outside of Rome today. The *Sacramentary,* a text of all the liturgical prayers and rituals, has taken its place and is used throughout the Church Universal for the celebration of the sacraments. The readings of the Mass, Gospels and Epistles, as well as the Psalms, are found in a liturgical text known as the *Lectionary.*

missionary a person, male or female, lay or religious, sent by the church with her full authority to minister to peoples in distant lands or nearer to home, to preach the Gospel (when deacons or priests), and by general acts and examples of evangelization.

missus dominicus a Latin phrase that translates to 'envoy of the ruler.' An unofficial diplomatic post in place from the high Middle Ages through to the early twentieth century used by emperors and kings as personal envoys to the pope, by-stepping the more formal diplomatic channels of the day. The papacy, in return, often sent laymen from the Papal Court as private envoys to monarchs when a pope likewise wished not to employ one of his cardinals (legates) or archbishops (nuncios) in these missions. These laymen were also referred to as a *missus dominicus.*

mistletoe an evergreen that for centuries has been the symbol of healing that originated in pagan Norse cultures centuries before Christianization of the people of Scandinavia. After Christianity arrived in the north of

Europe the church assigned the symbolic meaning of 'Divine Love' to mistletoe and from this developed the notion that mistletoe brought love to those who stood beneath it on the anniversary of Christ's birth.

monk the title of a male member of one of the monastic orders of the Catholic or Orthodox churches or in oriental cultures of men who enter a Buddhist temple for a period of one year.

Monseigneur the French equivalent to "monsignor' and 'monsignore' meaning 'my Lord.' In the French form it may be applied to either laymen of the highest social classes, particularly royal persons and to honorary members of the papal court. For a layman to make use of this honorific, the *lettres patent* (grant of title) by a king or emperor would have to specifically grant its use. Examples of its use in both forms would be *Monseigneur l'Evêque* (my lord the bishop) or *Monseigneur le Prince-Souverain* (My lord the Sovereign Prince).

monsignorial dignity, (original title-holders) originally only a few papal officials were entitled to the use of the courtesy title "Monsignor." The listing of these officials included: the college of the seven official Protonotaries Apostolic *de numero participantium* (which translates to 'the number of participants'); the Protonotaries *supra numero* (supernumerary), including, the canons of the three patriarchal basilicas of Rome and the canons of certain cathedral churches, while in office, and the members of the collegiate chapters in Rome; Protonotaries Apostolic *ad instar participantium* (which translates to 'after the manner of participants'), including the canons of certain additional named cathedral churches, and the *Ad Personam* Protonotaries (those named to the title by the pope without responsibilities). The title was also granted to the College of Auditors of Holy See; the college of officials of the Apostolic Camera; and the private chamberlains constituting the official college of pontifical masters of ceremonies as well as other prelates of the Roman Curia not members of any of the above named colleges.

Later the title was extended to the numerous domestic prelates (now referred to as Prelates of Honor of His Holiness) scattered throughout the dioceses of the world; to the official private chamberlains known as *participantes*; to the super-numerary private chamberlains (*camerieri segreti soprannumerari*), the honorary chamberlains in violet; the honorary chamberlains *extra urbem* (today known as "Chaplains of His Holiness); the official college of chaplains; the honorary private chaplains; the honorary chaplains *extra urbem*; the private clerics; and the official college of papal chaplains.

With the exception of the Protonotaries Apostolic, the Prelates of Honor and the Chaplains of His Holiness, none of the above offices and titles has survived the changes to the Papal Household mandated in 1968. See also: *Papal Honors for the Clergy.*

Mother General the title of the head of a religious order of women with full powers of governance under the terms of the constitution of that order or community. Today many have opted for the title 'Sister President' or merely "President' but this official church title has never been abolished. A Mother General may serve for life or for a set number of years. In conversation she is addressed as 'Reverend Mother' or familiarly as 'Mother'.

Mother, Reverend the courtesy title, or form of address, for the female head of a convent or other form of religious house of women.

Mother Superior the official title of a head of a religious house of women although it is seldom used today. This title refers to the head of a local house and not the head of the entire order or community.

Mother Vicar the title of the second in command to an abbess in a monastery of nuns. She may be elected or chosen by the reigning abbess and her term of office may be either for life or for a set period. Although she holds this title, she is traditionally addressed as 'Sister' followed by her professed name.

Mozarabic Rite the liturgical formula in use throughout Iberia, particularly Spain, Portugal and the Balearic Islands until The Second Vatican Council. It was also present in those places where Portugal and Spain established colonies.

muscarium an alternate title for the papal *flabellum.*

myron the term for the Holy Oils used in several of the Orthodox churches for their sacraments which always are made and blessed in the heart of Jerusalem.

narthex the vestibule of a large church. In St. Peter's Basilica this space is alternatively referred to as the *narthex*, *vestibule*, and *atrium*.

natalis from the Latin for birthday and known in English as 'Natal Day', the anniversary date of a baptized Christian's death. The custom of honoring the day that someone died began in ancient Rome when great festivals would be held for a deceased senator, dictator, or emperor. Coming into the church, the Natal Day of deceased popes, bishops, and saints began to be observed after the second century. Today, the pope honors his deceased predecessors in this way by celebrating a Mass in their honor at the Vatican. Likewise, the faithful throughout the world schedule a memorial Mass for a deceased family member on the anniversary date of death, and when new saints are canonized, typically the feast day date assigned them on the Roman calendar is that of their earthly death.

nave today the central aisle of a large multi-aisle church or cathedral. It is almost always wider than the other aisles. Originally, it included all of the space reserved for the people with the sanctuary being only a small apse-like alcove at the terminus of the nave. The name comes from the Latin word for 'bark' in reference to both the elongated shape of the barges of that time and in spiritual reference to Noah's Ark that contained all surviving life in the same way that the church contains those saved by their faith.

Ne Temere a decree of Pope-Saint Pius X that was later incorporated into the 1917 Code of Canon Law (remaining in effect until 1970) which empowered the bishops and priests of the world to strictly control the rights of a Catholic person wishing to enter into a mixed marriage, a union between a baptized Catholic and a non-Catholic Christian in most circumstances. This decree permitted the requirement that all children of this type union would have to baptized and raised as Roman Catholics and it empowered in some places the local pastor to require religious education of the non-Catholic partner before a marriage would be permitted in hope that this partner would eventually convert to Catholicism. The *Ne Temere* degree was latter revised and the requirements leading to the permissions for a mix marriage have been somewhat relaxed under the new code of canon law. During the years that it was enforced, many civil governments, including those in Canada, New Zealand, and Australia rose up in opposition to what they felt to be the prejudicial conditions of the decree.

niche a recessed opening in either the exterior or interior walls of a building common in the Renaissance and Baroque periods, sometimes used for decorative purposes or to hold statues.

nihil obstate a Latin title which translates to 'without objection' and which is first applied to all theological and liturgical works submitted to a bishop for the grant of *imprimatur;* a step taken once a work is approved by the Church. This approval is required for the publication of specific dogmatic works and before a bishop grants his formal approval. It falls to a local priest who must first study each text thoroughly to assure the authorities that it is free of all error. When this priest, known formally as the *censor Librorum* (translating to 'censor of texts') assures the bishop that there are no errors; the work is formally granted the *nihil obstate.* Consideration is then given to a further grant of the *imprimatur.*

Nomina of Catholic Saints the formal term applied to the list of male and female canonized saints from which the assigned dates for the celebration of feasts, memorials and solemnities are taken. The 'Nomina" is also the list from which Catholic parents are in theory supposed to take the names given to their newborn children at baptism.

Norman the style of Gothic ecclesiastical architecture found throughout England, Wales, and Ireland. It is so called because it was introduced into Great Britain at the time of the Norman Conquest. In every way, it is a pure example of early to mid-Gothic design. Typified by interior frills and a sense of light with a heavier exterior but one decorated, nevertheless, with the earliest elements of the coming high Gothic. Fine examples of this style exist throughout the United Kingdom as well as in North America where it was most popular with both Catholic and Anglican Church architects of the nineteenth and twentieth centuries: Canterbury Cathedral being one of the finest of examples of this style. It should be noted that almost all of these Norman churches in the U.K., both great cathedrals and village chapels, were all founded as Roman Catholic institutions and were all consecrated as such centuries before the Protestant Reformation.

novice a person, male or female, admitted into a religious order in the first stage of profession. A period of at least one year is required before the novice may move on to the next stage of admission but some orders require a more prolonged period of *novitiate*. In female orders, the novice is given the habit but the veil typically awarded is white.

nun correctly the title of a woman in a religious order where the solemnly professed vows of chastity, poverty and obedience are taken. Properly, a nun is a religious woman who has professed 'solemn vows' and lives by a monastic rule. Religious sisters, the hundreds of communities most familiar to Catholics the world over, are not technically nuns at all.

obelisk a single-stone giant monolith of Egyptian origins used for decorative purposes (but originally associated with mythical powers) that tapers at its peak to resemble the tip of a Egyptian pyramid. It is often found in Italianate church architecture and in crypt monuments in Catholic cemeteries.

oblate the term assumed in modern times by orders or communities at the time of their erection as a part of their formal title, such as the Oblates of Saint Francis de Sales but technically, this title applied to those who entered a monastic society early in life, without promise to enter the order, for the purpose of education or protection due to being orphaned. It meant 'to learn' and for this humble reasons was later applied to many orders of the modern era.

Observer, Permanent the title of the status granted in international diplomatic law to nations and non-governmental organizations that have been seated at the United Nations in New York, Geneva, and at its many offices throughout the world, and at international conferences throughout the world where nations formally gather, but that do not have the right to vote in the assembly of nations. The Holy See, a member-state of the United Nations Organization, chooses not to accept full standing with the right to vote so as not to be forced into taking a position on issues that may fall into diplomatic malaise or open belligerency. As such, they formally enjoy Permanent Observer status so that the papal representative may lobby all nations, on all sides, on issues that are important to the entire human family. Although they may not vote, this influence is most powerful. The Mission of the Holy See to the United Nations Organization at both New York and Geneva, and all others like it, is referred to as Permanent *Observership* rather than as an embassy.

Octave the term for an eight day long period of festival within the church. Originally, and coming into the church from the Hebraic traditions, all festivals extended for seven days but after the fourth century many were extended to include an extra day of prayer and celebration. It is believed that the Emperor Constantine the Great was the first to impose this extra day when he solemnly dedicated the Christian churches of Jerusalem and Tyre, an event that led to eight days of merriment. Today, the most well-known of the Octave feasts are Christmas and Easter.

omophorion an alternate title for the pallium; a term predominately used in the Orthodox churches especially as the design in these churches differs from the general Latin style pallium. In 2005, newly elected Pope Benedict XVI technically was invested as pope with a omophorion vs. the Latin pallium as Archbishop Piero Marini, Papal Master of Ceremonies, personally preferred this style and ordered its creation.

oratory technically, in Catholic architecture, a place reserved just for prayer, whereas a chapel could possess a reserved place for the Blessed Sacrament. But in time, the celebration of the Mass and the Divine Liturgy also were permitted. There are three types of oratories: the public oratory which are open for all the faithful; the semi-public oratory which may or may not be perpetually open to the public, and the private oratory such as those found in the home of a bishop or within a rectory.

Orders, Major the offices of Deacon, Priest and Bishop with the Office of Bishop being understood in theological terms as the "Fullness of Holy Orders." Major Orders use to also include the Office of Sub-Deacon, which no longer exists. Together these offices use to be known as the Sacred Orders.

Orders, Minor the offices of Lector, Acolyte in the post-Vatican II canons, with the Rite of Candidacy formally preparing a seminarian to be called to Holy Orders traditionally following the receipt of these two. The minor orders use to also include the offices of Porter, Lector, Exorcist, and Acolyte.

orphery the highly embroidered band that trims ecclesial vestments.

ossuary a stone container, usually of limestone or marble, that resembles a large ceremonial urn that was used to house the bones of a great saint. These ossuaries were traditionally enclosed within a wall or niche of a great church or basilica. The Constantinian basilica at the Vatican was filled with many such containers, however, it is unknown how many ossuaries now exist within the walls of the current, Renaissance St. Peter's.

Orthodox Church the numerous churches of the east that break from Rome at the time of the Eastern Schism or thereafter through numerous schisms within the Orthodox movement. Although independent of each other, the spiritual leader of the Orthodox remains the Patriarch of Constantinople.

Our Father See: *The Lord's Prayer.*

pace a small passage way in a Gothic church or a small aisle leading to an out of the way site within any other style church, such as to a hidden lavatory.

paenula an ancient Greek poncho that is said to be one of the forerunners of the modern Gothic-style chasuble or priest vestment.

palatine the term for all things associated with a palace such as a palatine chapel, palatine chaplain, palatine prelate, palatine guard, or palatine count.

pall, funeral the cloth traditionally placed over a casket during the funeral liturgy. Originally, the funeral pall was made of black cloth, symbolic of the sobriety of death, and on which was embroidered a large white cross. But after Vatican II, the symbolism of the church shifted from that of death to rebirth and baptism and thus the funeral cloth likewise changed. Thereafter, the funeral pall traditionally is made of white linen cloth or white damask. Christian emblems are also permitted upon it. Catholic protocol, however, permits the funeral pall's replacement for royal or noble dignitaries. In these instances, the church permits the substitution of the personal or family *heraldic standard* as the appropriate funereal vesture.

palm the use of blessed palm, or palm fronds, on Palm Sunday is one of the ancient sacramentals of the church. The palm is used to commemorate the historic entrance of Christ into Jerusalem. The palm is symbolic of the joy of the promise of salvation and victory over sin and death. Because of this symbolism, the church has assigned the palm to all martyrs as one of the symbols of their heroic deaths. Each year the palms are burned and with a mixture of holy oils become the ashes used on Ash Wednesday.

Palm Sunday known in Italian as *Domenica di Palma,* and in Latin as *Dies Palmarum,* the Sunday prior to Easter and thus the sixth and last Sunday of Lent. It is also the official start of Holy Week. As such, it is also the beginning of the penitential period referred to as the Easter duty. It comes into the church immediately after the first Pentecost as the memory of this historic day evoked great joy and pain, alike, amongst the surviving Apostles and Disciples of Christ. Once Constantine Christianized the empire in the fourth century, even the emperors carried palms in procession to re-enact this event. It became so venerated a feast that only Easter surpassed it on the liturgical calendar in both the East and West. The feast took many names but perhaps the Spanish, *paschua florida,* is the most noteworthy for it is under this title that the American state of Florida was later named. Palms are used throughout the Universal Church as they were in Jerusalem during Christ's triumphal entry into the city beginning His Passion and Death. During some periods of history, roses and other flowers were substituted for the palms strewn during the procession of the Palm Sunday Mass. This custom is no longer seen, however, in Rome (particularly at the Vatican) olive branches are most often substituted. In Bavaria they use large cattails, or swamp willow that are decorated with other flowers and silk bows. In some localities ornate braiding of palm fronds are created for the celebrants and the people and bishops often replace the crozier on this day with a large version of these ornate displays. Palm braidings are also used to decorate the graves of Catholic faithful in many parts of the world and smaller examples are proudly displayed within homes and on outer doors.

panegyric the term applied to a public speech of praise for an esteemed or famous person. Although this speech may be for the living, it is more often applied to the dead. The word 'panegyric' comes to us from the Greek and translates to 'fit for the ears of the general public'. It is similar to but not exactly the same as 'eulogy' and is most often applied to remarks made at a high churchman's funeral rites.

papacy the generic term applied to all functions and actions of the Petrine Office. It is also the term used to describe the tenure of a specific pope.

particular church the canonical, or legal, term applied to an ecclesial family, or community, found in one of two forms: the first of these is by way of the *local church* meaning a community headed by a bishop, archbishop or other prelate of similar rank and which are typically called the *dioceses* or *archdioceses.* In this form is also found jurisdictions such as the *abbey-nullius* or *territorial*, the *apostolic prefectures* and the *apostolic vicariates* all of which owe obedience to the Holy See at Rome. The second form of particular church are the various Rites of the Catholic Church such as the Latin Rite, the Byzantine, and all the other Eastern churches in communion with Rome. This latter category is referred to collectively as the *sui juris* or autonomous churches in Catholicism. These are headed by patriarchs and/or major archbishops but owe ultimate allegiance to the pontiff at Rome.

passion plays the reenactment of the Passion, Death and Resurrection of Jesus Christ which originated in the liturgy of Holy Week and which sprang forth in the Middle Ages. It is most commonly found in central Europe, South American and in the Philippines.

pastor the official of the church that governs a parish. Church law requires that they be the foremost teachers of the faith within their jurisdiction and they must become the servant of the sacraments and liturgy of the church there as well. The title pastor generally translates to shepherd and it is this understanding of the pastor's role that the church chooses to foster most of all.

patriarchal basilicas the title long-enjoyed by all of the major basilicas of Rome and several other major basilicas under papal benefice to set them apart from all others of similar rank but not enjoying association with the Petrine Office. In December 2006, Pope Benedict XVI stripped the patriarchal title from St. Peter's Basilica as a gesture of goodwill towards the Patriarch of Constantinople and the Orthodox Church that long felt the Roman use of these titles encroached upon their own rights and privileges long associated with the patriarchal dignity. This move by the pope caused great concern inside the church but it is assumed that further patriarchal titles will be dropped in future.

Patriarch, Ecumenical the highest title of the prelate elected to govern the Greek Orthodox Church.

Patriarch of the West a papal title denoting that the popes had universal spiritual jurisdiction throughout the known world and which formed a part of the formal litany of titles and offices held by each Roman Pontiff. In 2006 Pope Benedict XVI stripped the Petrine Office of this ancient title, citing it as being offensive to the current Orthodox brethren that claim exclusive use to the patriarchal dignity. Although this caused consternation within the curia and throughout the church, Pope Benedict made it clear that this move was intended as a symbolic form of outreach to separated Christians.

PAX from the Latin for 'peace' an ornate wall or table plaque in the Renaissance or Baroque style that depicts various devotional images which were used to inspire the people. The most common form of the PAX is found in the Stations of the Cross devotional tablets affixed to the interior walls in churches designed prior to 1965. Originally these plaques were made in gold or silver and were portable so that in the Tridentine form of the Mass when the rite of peace was introduced the celebrating priest would kiss one of these devotional scenes before it was carried to each of the non-celebrating clergy present to do the same. In Italy the PAX were known as *gli tabelle pacis* (peace tablets). They are also commonly known as *retablo.*

This term 'pax' was also applied to the actual rite of peace within the liturgy and was taken from the words *Pax tecum* which translates to 'peace be with you' which the celebrant imparts on other ministers of the Mass.

They would respond with the word '*et cum Spiritu tuo*' which in English is rendered as either '*and with your spirit*' or '*and also with you.*'

peculiar, pontifical the former term for the current canonical status of 'Immediately Subject to the Holy See' pertaining mainly to dioceses but also applied to abbeys, canonries, and other ecclesial institutes; an entity with no superiors other than the pope.

peculiar, royal an ancient Catholic Church title that after the Protestant Reformation, and in particular after the establishment of the Church of England, fell into abeyance, but which was immediately assumed as one of its own by the Anglican hierarchy. It refers to a chapel with a full chapter of canons headed by a dean that was not subject to the local bishop. Rather, it was fully independent of all ecclesiastical authority, being immediately subject to the monarch who considered these places to be his own personal royal chapel. In Catholic monarchies this institution, and similar privileges, was quite common and to this day, Catholic monarchs maintain the right to submit names for the *terna,* the list of proposed new bishops for dioceses in their nations, and also often have the right to nominate new canons for their cathedrals. There are no existing Roman Catholic royal peculiars, however, many Anglican institutions exist still in the United Kingdom—nearly all of these founded as Roman Catholic institutions centuries ago. The most famous of these royal peculiars is Saint George's Chapel, Windsor Castle.

pediment a large triangular device used for ornamentation at the end of a roofline (so that the exposed edge does not appear without ornamentation) as in the case of the terminus of Bernini's colonnade in Rome. These devices are also used architecturally atop windows and doors to add interest.

Penance one of the seven sacraments of the church, today known properly as the Sacrament of Reconciliation.

Pentecost known in the original Greek as *Penteskostes,* meaning the fiftieth day, the solemn feast commemorating the decent of the Holy Spirit upon the surviving Apostles and the Blessed Virgin Mary. This event came into the church as early as the Apostolic age, noteworthy from the outset of Christianity because of the great impact that this sacramental moment had on all those present. As its title suggests, the feast of Pentecost comes close to the fiftieth day after Easter. Like so many of our feasts, this celebration was originally Jewish in nature, a feast coming fifty days after the closing of the Passover commemoration. It is unlikely that the actual descent of the Holy Spirit took place exactly fifty days after the resurrection but it is likely that the Apostles and the Virgin Mary did gather at that time as Jewish custom would have mandated as and they were fearful of retribution, would have done so secretly and together. For this reason, and as Scripture places it so, the church places the Pentecost event at the fiftieth day after Easter. This day was also once known as, Whitsunday, especially in English speaking nations, because on this day many converts were baptized wearing the traditional white garments of this sacrament. The Anglican Church continues to refer to this feast as Whitsunday but the Roman Church has not done so for many years.

perdurante munere a definition applied in the church to a posting or appointment that is more than honorary; to be said to be more or less an assignment on a permanent basis. The clearer translation of the term would be 'an office lasting or enduring for a long time.' An example of a current usage for this term is those extra-ordinary members appointed to the Pontifical Academies.

Peritus a title used in the church primarily for theologians who serve as experts on theological and ecclesial matters most typically at Ecumenical Councils such as the Second Vatican Council (1963-65). Pope Benedict XVI served as a peritus for the then Archbishop of Cologne at the Second Vatican Council. The term translates in English to 'expert'.

Persian Rite Another name of the Syriac rite.

per substitute a Latin title representing a grant of powers by the pope to another to govern a specific office, congregation, or church as a prelate would see fit so to do with full rights of jurisdiction over it even though the title to govern it is held by another. One such grant was given to Cardinal Ludovico Ludovisi in 1621 when the pope permitted him the right *per substitute* to interfere in the inner workings of the Roman Curia offices even though this right was normally the pope's alone and even though cardinal-prefects headed each of these offices with the right to fully govern them.

petasos a round, large brimmed hat originating in Greece from which derived the Roman sombrero and from which, in turn, developed the *galero,* the hat of cardinals and other greater prelates.

Peter's Pence the annual international collection, begun by King Canute of England in the eleventh century, that benefits the operation of the Holy See and the upkeep of the Vatican Basilica. It was not until the last century, however, that all funds gathered in this collection made their way to Rome. More typically, this annual collection remained at home to be used for special projects approved by the papacy, such as the construction of new abbeys or monasteries or new cathedrals.

Today, the Holy See greatly depends upon the funds collected each year in the *Peter's Pence* collection for the upkeep of the Roman Curia and St. Peter's Basilica.

Petrine Office the English language phrase used to define the papacy as the sole office formally erected by Saint Peter, Prince of the Apostles, and from which thereafter succeeded all authority of the Vicar of Christ in the person of each succeeding pontiff.

Pfarrkirche the German title for a parish church and when this title follows the German word *kathedrale* it refers to the cathedral of a dioceses also serving as a canonical parish. Normally, a cathedral should not serve as a parish as it is intended as the bishop's seat and the place where all in a diocese may feel welcome and thus stands apart from the limitations of a canonical parish.

piazza a large square or plaza found in front of cathedrals, basilicas, palaces, and public buildings used for ceremonies and as a place for crowds to gather; a great public space such as the esplanades in front of the Marian shrines at Fatima and Lourdes.

pilaster a column-like device extending from the wall. The style of a pilaster usually mimics the choice of the order of columns (i.e. Doric, Ionic, Corinthian, etc.) employed throughout the church.

Pileus qaudratus the original Latin name for the *Biretta*.

pilgrimages the pious act of the faithful seeking a closer union with God through a spiritual and physical journey to a site approved by the Church as an authentic shrine of mercy, forgiveness, or religious enrichment. Such places must be approved by the Holy See and usually carry the award of an indulgence with completion of the *pilgrimage* ritual.

The earliest formal *pilgrimages* approved by the Church were to the Holy Land. This journey was difficult, time consuming and dangerous for the faithful. Many never returned. It was popularized by the Empress Helena, mother of Constantine the Great, who in the fourth century traveled to Jerusalem to follow in the footsteps of Jesus' public life. It was during this *pilgrimage* that the empress found items of the Passion directly associated with Christ, including the *True Cross* and the steps from Pontius Pilate's palace, which Christ climbed after the scouring at the pillar. Helena returned to Rome with all that she had discovered included the *True Cross* and the steps, which have been built into a small palace across from the Basilica of St. John Lateran. Visits to this pilgrim site, now known as the *Scala Santa* (or Holy Stairs), climb each step on their knees, praying for the mercy and the good of the souls in Purgatory as they do so. The most popular pilgrim sites today, however, remain the Marian Shrines at Lourdes and Fatima.

pillar a vertical architectural device used for real support. Pillars may be fully rounded, square in shape, or multi-sided.

pittacia along with the ampullæ one of the two vessels used to conserve the holy oils used in the sacramental life of the church.

plafond a flat ceiling found in Romanesque or more modern church architecture, typically embellished with gold or paint.

Plainchant the simple mode of chant used exclusively in the church until polyphony ascended as the preeminent mode of sacred music in the ninth century.

pontificalia the term for all of the vestments and insignia unique to the office of bishop. Sometimes also referred to commonly (but incorrectly) as 'pontificals'.

Pontifical Academies those institutions established at Rome as senior advisory bodies for the popes. There are ten in number, the most famous being the Pontifical Academy of Sciences founded in 1603 to promote the advancement of scientific learning. The most recent creations came in 1994, created by Pope John Paul II, under the titles of the Pontifical Academy of Social Sciences and the Pontifical Academy for Life. The remaining academies concern themselves with Tomistics (the philosophic science of the scholastic method of Saint Tomas Aquinas), Theology, Sacred Archeology, Fine Arts, Marian Theology, and the Pontifical Academies of the Immaculate Conception and for Martyriology (the study of Martyrs). The most brilliant men and women, regardless of religious affiliation, in each discipline are appointed to the appropriate academy under the title of Pontifical Academician, a posting nearly as prestigious as the Nobel Prize. Each pontifical academician is given this lifetime appointment as well as the title of 'Excellency.'

Pontifical Ecclesiastical Academy the title of one of the most prestigious colleges in Rome, originally entitled the *Pontifical Academy for Noble Ecclesiastics*. Not one of the pontifical academies set up through the centuries to advise popes on particular disciplines (*see above*), the Pontifical Ecclesiastical Academy was originally founded for the sons of princes, dukes, counts, and diplomats so that these young men could prepare to enter Holy Orders apart from non-titled persons. As these men typically rose quickly to the heights of the church's hierarchy, this college also became associated with training for the papal diplomatic service. Today, all priests are eligible for admittance into the academy regardless of social standing, but one must possess a doctorate in sacred theology and must be prepared to enter a doctoral program for canon law as well as the study of numerous languages. Each candidate must be personally nominated by his bishop to one of the limited seats available each year. As such, only the brightest young priests are ever posted to this prestigious institution and from it come the finest future papal diplomats and curialists. Very few of these priests return to diocesan or parish work.

pope-mobile the name applied to one of a number of white conversion vehicles owned by the Vatican that are part 'sport utility vehicle' (SUV) and part parade display unit. Each is fitted with an elevated glass enclosed rear section, which is reserved for the seating of the pope and his closest aides so that the people can easily see them. As the section used by the pontiff is well lit and elevated, many more can see him than when other vehicles were used.

There are several 'pope-mobiles' in existence, some at the Vatican and others in museums in places where the pope once visited. The first pope-mobiles were merely open trucks used by John Paul II, Servant of God, during his first visits to Mexico and Poland. And today one or more open versions still exist. John Paul II was on one of these when he was shot in Saint Peter's Square and Pope Benedict continues to make use of one after the Wednesday General Audience at the Vatican in warm weather. Several automobile manufactures have made a gift of a 'pope-mobile' to the Vatican, the most recent being one presented by Mercedes-Benz to German born Pope Benedict XVI.

portal the term applied to the largest door(s) of an important state or church building such as the main entranceways into most cathedrals, including St. Patrick's in New York that are made of ornate bronze.

portantina the enclosed version of the *sedia gestatoria* reserved for the popes. It was carried aloft by four men and resembled an enclosed carriage without wheels. It was retired at the time of the First World War but a fine example of one may be found in the Lateran Museum Collection. The portantina was the original precursor to the *Pope-Mobile.*

portico an open space on the façade, or front, of a building that extends forward and is covered by a roof or upper floor so that people or carriages (now automobiles) can pass within it.

post communion the conclusion of the Liturgy of the Eucharist and the liturgical action leading into the final prayers and blessing at the conclusion of the Mass.

postulant the title for one who enters religious life. The first stage before one enters the novitiate.

poverty, evangelical the renunciation in the Christian Counsels of all or partial ownership in material goods.

praepositus the Latin title meaning 'Provost' which is a title used in the Catholic Church for officials in chapters of canons, in the diocesan curia, for superiors in certain religious orders and for persons in the administration of Catholic universities.

prebend see *benefice.*

precedence, episcopal the official table of precedence for bishops of the church has varied through the centuries and also has varied by Rite. In the Latin Rite, precedence is given first to Major Archbishops, then to Archbishop-Primates, to Archbishops and to Bishops. Archbishops within their rank or class are now seated by date of consecration as are bishops within their own rank or class but this was not always the case. In the early church, bishops were typically seated according to their personal age (a custom that originated in the church in North Africa) and in the East it was by the historical nature of the See that a prelate occupied that precedence was granted. In Europe, precedence was muddled even further when the incumbent was also born a prince or nobleman. Rome altered this for the Latin Rite in the early twentieth century. Although the Orthodox churches continue to grant precedence by the history of the See (especially a patriarchate) that a prelate occupies, the west more or less now recognizes prelates by rank or class and then by date of consecration.

predella the top step, or platform, on which is placed the fixed altar.

prefect apostolic an ecclesiastical title seldom used today that denotes a cleric that has been charged with the governance of a territory that has not as yet been erected into a full diocese. The church sometimes prefers the title of *prelate apostolic* for those governing such territories.

prelate a cleric who has been elevated to high office in the Church, such as abbot, bishop, archbishop, patriarch or cardinal. The Holy See also awards honorary titles to some clerics because of the post that they hold or the accomplishments that they have achieved. These *honorary prelates* are the monsignors, archimandrites, and chorbishops of the Latin and Oriental Rites.

prelati palatini also known as the *prelati di fiochetto,* the four highest non-episcopal functionaries of the old Papal Court abolished by Paul VI in 1969. These four officials (later only three), were entitled to the style of 'Excellency' and enjoyed various added privileges of rank, vesture and heraldry. They came to be know by the Roman slang, prelates of the fiochetto, because these clerics were entitled to dress their horses and carriages with tassels, or fiocchi. These four officers managed the Petrine Office and the pageantry of the popes of old and were considered amongst the most important in church government because of their close proximity to the pope. The four offices were: the *Majordomo, Maestro di Camera, Master of the Sacred Palace* and the *Papal Auditor.* Each of the four were always Protonotaries Apostolic de Numero, and in fact formed the actual College of Protonotaries at the Vatican.

presbytery the place between the chancel and the apse once reserved as seating for special clergy (also known as presbyters), from which this area takes its name.

presepio the Italian term sometimes also spelt as *presipio* from the Latin meaning 'to instruct' and used in Italy to describe the Manger, or Nativity, scenes at Christmas. In Italy, these tend to be very elaborate tableau more baroque in design than reminiscent of the Holy Land with dozens of figurines presenting an entire village. The Nativity or Manger scene was invented by Saint Francis of Assisi in the thirteenth century as a way of teaching the peasants about the birth of the Christ child. He used living participants dressed in local clothing so as to illustrate the scriptural narrative in a manner most easily understood by the ignorant people of that time. The term *presepio a vivere* is the title for a Nativity scene using living figures.

prie-dieu a kneeler used in the church, most often decorated with Christian symbols and including a place, or shelf, where the user may deposit a prayer book or Bible. Also used by believers in their homes.

priest the second in the Major Orders of deaconate, priesthood and the episcopacy. The term comes to us from the Greek, *prebuteros,* meaning a man of great learning and wisdom. Originally, the New Testament texts employ this usage for elders that govern rather than for persons associated with the liturgy. For this office the texts used the Greek term, *hiereus,* from which we get the modern word, hierarchy. In time, the term presbyter came to represent the office of priesthood as we now understand it. Collectively, as a body, men in the Office of Priest are said to be members of the presbyterate or priesthood.

primate the senior-most archbishop of a nation, sometimes because the diocese over which he governs is the oldest, or first, in that place. The diocese of a primate is known as a *primatial see.* Highest precedence and other honors are always accorded to this archbishop when the local Church gathers as a whole such as in Poland where the primate if only an archbishop is permitted to vest in the scarlet of a cardinal. The Pope is the primate of Italy and the Archbishop of Baltimore is the *de facto* primate of America (honorary primate) because Baltimore was the first archdiocese in the United States. Other Primatial titles are Lyon in France, Armagh as primate of All Ireland (although Dublin is known as Primate of Ireland), Esztergom for Hungary, Toledo in Spain and Quebec as primate of Canada amongst many others both active and defunct. Primates in the Catholic Church follow patriarchs and major archbishops in precedence but precede metropolitan archbishops and titular archbishops of all ranks and offices. The title of primate is also used similarly in the Church of England, with the Archbishop of Canterbury as Primate of All England and the Archbishop of York as Primate of England, and in the Orthodox churches where the title is assumed by the patriarchs who head one of the independent churches.

Primatial See the jurisdiction held by a primate but not in an Ad Personam manner. Examples of the primatial see would be Lyon (France) as Primatial See of all the Gauls; Toledo as Primatial See of Spain; Quebec as Primatial See of Canada; and Baltimore as Primatial See of the United States (although the latter is a historical, but not formally recognized, designation).

primatial cathedral the proper title of the cathedral of the primate of a nation or local church. As such, an example of the proper title would be: 'The Primatial Cathedral of the Annunciation.'

primicerius a Latin title used in the Church that equates to the modern usage of the title of 'Rector-Primus', a post in which one is set apart to govern a church institution without wider powers such as that of bishop, vicar general, or abbot.

primus inter pares the Latin term for 'first amongst equals,' a phrase applied to both the clergy and to persons of royal rank. For instance, the pope is accorded the position of 'primus inter pares' amongst the world's emperors, kings, princes and presidents in terms of sovereign status. He is likewise the 'first amongst equals' in the college of bishops in the Catholic Church. The primates of the world are 'first amongst equals' within their own nations. In the Orthodox family, the Patriarch of Constantinople (Istanbul), known properly as the *Ecumenical Patriarch*, is 'primus inter pares' amongst all the patriarchs of Orthodoxy.

prince-abbot a title once enjoyed by certain abbots in the Holy Roman Empire that simultaneously ruled as the feudal lord of the territory surrounding the abbey. The ecclesial equivalent of this office is *abbot nullius*, a rank in the prelature wherein the abbot of an important abbey simultaneously governs the church of the region surrounding the abbey with the same responsibilities of a residential bishop.

Prince-bishop, prince archbishop the titles of high churchmen who simultaneously governed a secular principality which had earlier come into the domain of the church in addition to their ecclesial state of a diocese or archdiocese. In the Holy Roman Empire these clerics were entitled to vote for the next emperor.

prince-provost a title similar to that of prince-abbot but found in monasteries of those religious houses where the superior was entitled 'provost' in place of 'abbot' such as at the Augustinian abbey at Salzburg. The title of provost was combined with the titular of prince when a son of a princely house of the Holy Roman Empire rose to the rank of superior within such a monastery.

prior the head of a convent of men in some religious orders wherein that community as a whole is known as a *priory.* The female equivalent in these orders is known as a *prioress.*

priory a religious house, or monastery, of either men or women headed by a prior (or prioress). There are two forms: the independent, or conventual, priory in which the prior reports to no superior and the obedient priory which is governed by a prior that reports to an abbot of a superior abbey.

private docent an honorary title conferred on academics who have already earned a doctoral degree in one discipline but who has gained competence in another and who thusly seeks the right to teach in both. To achieve this title, abbreviated in post-nominal form as *P.D.*, an academic must publish writings in the secondary topic and must present a formal lecture before judges in this discipline. Today this honorary position is most commonly found in German and Austrian academic institutions.

profession proclamation the words spoken by an abbot or abbess within the cloister of a monastery or abbey over a newly professed monk, friar, or nun completing the years-long process of preparation that culminates in the solemn profession of the *Evangelical Counsels.* The formula varies within each order of men and women but relies on a standard format for canonical inspiration such as: *"And I (the abbot or abbess), on the part of God Almighty, promise you (the newly professed), if you observe all of this faithfully, life everlasting. In the name of the Father, and of the Son, and of the Holy Spirit. Amen!"* After these words are proclaimed, the newly professed takes his/her place as a permanent member of the monastic or mendicant community.

pro hac vice the Latin phrase translating to 'for the time being' and used by the church to qualify an action taken for the short term. For instance, when Cardinal Andrez Deskur was promoted from the title of the Roman diaconal church of S. Caesarea in Palatio to the class of cardinal-priest, he wished to retain his original diaconal appointment rather than to transfer to another Roman parish and so with his elevation came the formal title of Cardinal-Priest in the title of S. Caesarea in Palatio *pro hac vice* (meaning that this church remains a diaconal church but for the time being has been elevated to a presbyteral title).

promoveatur ut amoveatur the Latin phrase that literally translates to 'may he be promoted so that he shall be removed' but which more or less in modern parlance translates to 'up and out' in regards to removing a troublesome churchman. For more than eight hundred years the church has used this phrase when a pope or high church official needed to rid himself of a lower ranking cleric. It long ago became the philosophy of the church to promote a rival or unwanted cleric to a much higher rank and position so that at the same time he would be removed from the pope's presence. Most often, although this transfer carried with it higher honors, it seldom carried with it substantial power. It was the Catholic Church of the Middle Ages that perfected the custom of removing rivals by honoring them before transferring them. In such a way, the cleric to be removed saves face and it can never be said that he was attacked by his superiors as one day he may return to greatness himself. This custom is still very much in place today although it is seldom mentioned publicly.

Protocol, Chef de the title given by governments to the senior official responsible for maintaining the ceremonies attached to the receipt of foreign heads of states and governments as well as the person charged with regulating the accreditation and ceremonies attached to the diplomatic corps resident in the host capital. The Holy See likewise maintains an official for this purpose, entitled *cappo di protocollo,* who is traditionally a monsignor or bishop and who reports directly to the Cardinal-Secretary of State. The Vatican chief of protocol also interfaces with the Prefect of the Papal Household and the Papal Master of Ceremonies in the exercise of his responsibilities.

Protodeacon the title given to the senior most Cardinal-Deacon of the Church; the churchman given the privilege of announcing the election of a new pope from the central loggia of S. Peter's Basilica (known as the *Habemus Papam* proclamation) and as such the prelate that announces to the world the name of that new pope. The Eastern Rites of the Catholic Church, as well as the Orthodox Communion, make use of this title as an honorific for the senior deacon (traditionally a married man) within each ecclesial jurisdiction.

Protopresbyter the title given to the senior most Cardinal-Priest of the Church who has assumed this position because he has served longer than any other member in the current College of Cardinals in the office of Cardinal-Priest. Historically, the church assigned to the *protopresbyter* as his own church in Rome is *San Lorenzo in Lucina*, a minor basilica that was originally a fourth century residence dedicated to St. Lawrence the Deacon and Martyr.

Protonotaries Apostolic also known as *Prothonotaries Apostolic. (*See *Chapter on Monsignorial titles).*

Protopope a title found primarily within the Orthodox churches but sometimes found in one or more of the Byzantine rites of the Roman Catholic Church meaning the senior priest after the bishop of the place in the same way that the Latin church uses the titles of Archpriest or Provost.

Protosincellus a diocesan official of the Maronite Rite equal to the post of Vicar General in the Latin Rite.

provincial the post in some of the more ancient orders of both men and women religious that governs a region, or ecclesiastical province, of that community. The provincial is responsible to the superior general of that order.

provost from the Latin, *prœpositus,* the senior official of a chapter of canons. In some places the term is Dean of the Chapter but in reality the provost title is superior to that of *decanus*(dean). In the first millennium, each diocese had a chapter and governing it was the local bishop followed by the archpriest of the chapter and then the archdeacon. When the bishop was outside the See, the archpriest assumed responsibilities for the diocese in the same way the Vicar General does today. At the same time, when the bishop was away, the governance of the chapter fell to the archdeacon. In those days the archpriest was referred to as the dean and the archdeacon as the provost.

In places where a chapter of canons still exists, the Holy See appoints the provost and the dean and the right to assist the bishop falls to the provost. It is also the right of the provost to administer the Last Rites to a dying bishop and it is his right to also preside at his burial. This title also has other meanings as well—all formed in understanding the important ecclesiastical role of the *prœpositus.* These include the role of academic provost, the high official charged with governing the curriculum of a university and thus a senior advisor of the president or chancellor, the person appointed to preside at important state or royal occasions, the grand steward of a large manor house or palace, the highest public official of a medieval district, or the mayor of ancient towns or villages in England, France, Germany and Spain. It is said that the incumbent in this title holds a *provostship.*

Psalter also known properly as the *Psalterium,* the collection of the psalms in a special order so as to be used by the Church in the Divine Liturgy.

Quarantore the historic term for the *Forty Hours Devotion* begun in the cathedral of Milan in 1537. The Blessed Sacrament is exposed in solemn form, usually in either a monstrance or ostensorium, for the veneration and worship by the faithful of a certain place for a period of forty uninterrupted hours during which time the Blessed Sacrament is never alone. At the beginning of the devotion, a Solemn Mass of Exposition is sung while at the conclusion of this period the Mass of Deposition is celebrated after which everyone present leaves the church in silence. This custom came to the church in North America through Bishop (now Saint) John Neumann of Philadelphia, born in Bohemia, who was a Redemptorist priest with great affection to this particular devotion. It soon spread beyond the borders of the church of Philadelphia and now is esteemed in Canada and the United States as much as it is in Europe. In some dioceses of the world, such as in Rome and in Philadelphia, this devotion has been perpetually observed for centuries—with one parish in those dioceses after another, in an unbroken time line, hosting the devotion.

quire an Old English word for 'choir' meaning the place in the chancel reserved for the canons and other ecclesiastics.

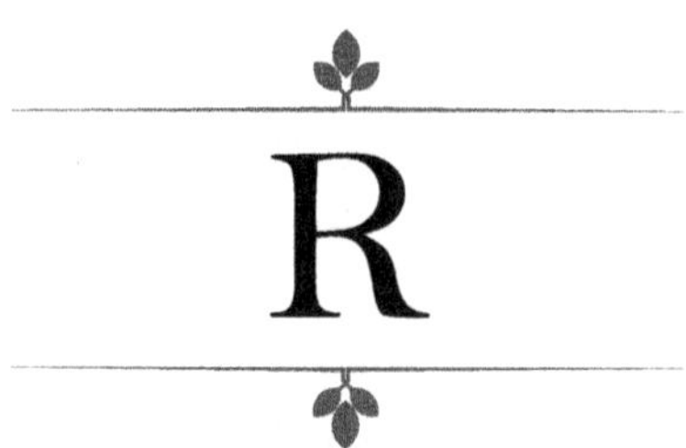

rabbi meaning 'teacher', the title used by the Apostles when addressing Christ. Also, a leader of the modern Jewish synagogues and temples.

Reason, age of a theological understanding of the point in human development when an individual becomes mature enough to understand the difference between right and wrong and to be morally responsible for one's own actions. The church and society in general set this age at or about the year seven.

rector in ecclesiastical terms, from the Latin, *regere,* meaning to govern, the title of a special pastor. In the pre-Vatican II period, this title was applied mainly to heads of jurisdictional missions but from time immemorial, the title of rector has also been assumed by the pastor of the cathedral parish (when the cathedral of a diocese is not separated from a jurisdictional parish at the same place). In these cases, still in effect today, the rector of these cathedrals is properly referred to as the 'Rector-Primus' (meaning first, or foremost, pastor of a diocese). A retired rector is known as the 'Rector-Emeritus' and the senior assistant to a parish rector is known as the 'Vice Rector' in so much as this title has been official conferred on him by the local bishop.

This title also enjoys a non-diocesan meaning as well. Some presidents of prestigious Catholic universities, such as the Lateran and the Gregorian Universities in Rome, are granted the title of 'Rector Magnificus' in place of the more traditional title of chancellor or president and the former governors of the various states that comprised the papal kingdom (i.e. Papal States) were granted the title of rector followed by the name of the place governed—such as '*rector Assisiensis*'—the title used in the Papal States for the civil governor of Assisi.

recusancy the formal term applied in England to all Roman Catholic families, particularly noble families, who refused to accept the established Church of England after the Protestant Reformation. Individuals are said to be *recusant* when they remain Catholic in officially Anglican England. The most famous example of a recusant family is the Howards to which the dukes of Norfolk belong. Lately the queen's cousin-in-law, the Duchess of Kent, has been referred to as 'the recusant duchess' because she had converted to Catholicism in 1994 but the term generally is addressed to those clans and families that never embraced Anglicanism.

refectory the church title for the common dinning room in monasteries, abbeys, convents, and seminaries. Meals are taken in common in a liturgical setting whereas prayers, litanies, and hymns accompany the taking of the meal.

relic a part of the body, such as bones, skin, or hair, also clothing or other personal items directly attributed to the use of a proclaimed saint of the Church. These sacred remains and associated items are traditionally venerated by the faithful. Actual bodily remains are considered 'First Class' relics. Clothing segments and other items that actually touched a saint's body at some time are known as 'Second Class' relics while something touched to second class items, such as new clothe not directly associated with the saint during his/her lifetime, are termed 'Third Class' relics.

reliquary the repository, sometimes ornately decorated, to hold relics of the saints of the Church. Sometimes multiple saint's relics are housed in one reliquary. In some important basilicas and cathedrals, an entire side chapel is dedicated to one particular saint and where numerous relics have been placed on display. Inside the Vatican Basilica of St. Peter's *reliquary-chapels* were built into each of the four great pylons supporting the massive dome, each dedicated to a particular saint and each containing that saint's relics.

rererdos a carved wooden, or stone screen built above and behind the high altars of medieval and renaissance cathedrals and larger churches. These screens typically stretched from wall to wall across the chancel, some containing richly carved images of the saints, and were erected from the floor rather than from on top of the altar of sacrifice. Those depicting a richly carved crucifix or crucifixion tableau are known as *Holy Rood* screens.

Retable, retablo a freestanding decorative altarpiece similar to a *reredos* but which is erected on top of an altar rather than from behind it. These devices became most popular in the late Renaissance although they have been in use in some places from the early Middle Ages. They are no longer erected as the altar of sacrifice now is normally freestanding and faces the people. *See also:* PAX.

Rituale Romanum also known as the Roman Ritual a compellation of all the rites, services, and sacraments of the church.

rogito a formal document baring the arms and insignia of a prelate and a curriculum vitae of both his personal information and his accomplishments as a churchmen that is placed inside the casket before burial so that in the event of beatification or canonization the facts of his life and service in the Church would be immediately known.

rosary officially known as the 'Most Holy Rosary of the Blessed Virgin Mary,' one of the most well known forms of prayer, and the foremost of the sacramentals, of the Catholic Church; a formula prayer established by Saint Dominic de Guzman in the early thirteenth century as a spiritual gift from the Blessed Virgin. The title comes from the Latin, *rosarium,* meaning rose wreath as from the beginning the devotion resembled such. It consists of beads, or knotted cords, consisting of a number of *Pater Nosters* and *Ave Marias* in a repetition similar to prayers in other religions. As the modern Ave Maria did not come into general use until after St. Dominic's death, the original rosary was substantially different than we know it today.

The modern rosary consists of three decades. In total there are six large beads representing the Pater Nosters and fifty-three smaller beads for counting the Ave Marias. Further, one additional large bead for a final Pater and three smaller ones for additional Aves were added in the fourteenth century. Some of the religious orders adopted a fifteen-decade rosary (vs. the standard three-decade design) and others customized rosaries of various other sizes, but these are traditionally mandated for use within the order only. Although all rosaries include one form of the crucifix or another, they may or may not also include numerous devotional medals, especially within religious orders and for those made to be worn on religious habits.

Four themes have been set aside for mental contemplation of the rosary. These include the historic three: the Joyful Mysteries in Christ's life, the Sorrowful Mysteries in Christ's Life, and the Glorious Mysteries. In his Apostolic Letter *Rosarium Virginis Mariæ* (2002), Pope John Paul II, Servant of God, ordered the addition of five new decades under the spiritual theme entitled 'Mysteries of Light.' This was the first time in six hundred years that such an addition had taken place and in his decree, the late pope reinforced the efficacy of contemplative prayer and of the power of the rosary devotion. John Paul likewise stated that the additional prayers not heretofore a formal part of the rosary would henceforth be considered so. Despite its age, or perhaps because of it, the rosary remains the most popular form of prayer in the Catholic Church to this day.

Contrary to popular belief, only the Pater Noster and the Ave Marias are required to complete a rosary. The addition of the 'Creed', the 'Glory Be', the 'Hail Holy Queen' and other subsequent devotional prayers are not necessary to successfully complete the devotion and to achieve the attached indulgence.

Of the rosaries created by religious orders that differ from the design in general use, the following are the most well known: the Little Chaplet of the Immaculate Conception, the Beads of the Blessed Sacrament, the Franciscan rosary, the Five Wounds rosary, and the Crown of our Savior rosary. Since the pontificate of Pope John Paul II, Servant of God, the papal rosary differs in that the crucifix used is in the image of that found atop the papal staff (crozier) and oftentimes bears both the papal coat of arms and his effigy as well. These are freely given as gifts to those that meet the pope. The rosary is the most favored sacramental carried by Catholic brides and it is included more than any other in the burial of Catholic faithful.

rubrics from the Latin, *rubrica,* meaning red. Taken from the red clay of the Roman district that carpenters used to mark the line needed prior to cutting sharp edges, thus translating to the need for precision. In the church the term has come to mean the rules or regulations governing some aspect of church law, custom, tradition or liturgical practice. So long as a rubric remains in affect, the church considers these rules to be sacrosanct and thus mandated for general and specific use throughout the Universal Church. There are many forms of rubric: the rubrics of the Mass, informing the celebrant(s) and the people of how the celebration of the liturgy shall proceed (and how it may not); the rubrics of the Liturgy of the Hours with the same purpose but specifically for the exercise of the Divine Liturgy, and the rubrics for the episcopal rituals for the proper exercise of the ceremonial life of the bishops. There are other collections of rubrics in good standing as well, the most famous of these being the *rubrica alraldica* which comprises more than six hundred and fifty currently rules governing the heraldry of the Roman Catholic Church.

Sacraments Baptism, Confirmation, Holy Eucharist, Penance/ Reconciliation, Matrimony, the Anointing of the Sick, and Holy Orders. The outward signs of the church of inner Divine Grace instituted by Christ Himself for the sanctification of mankind.

Sacramental, Liturgical the book used by the clergy during Sacred Liturgies presenting the formula for the celebration of the Mass and other liturgies including the Canons of the Mass, the orations, blessings and prayers.

sacramentals practices, customs, and devotions that help sanctify the Christian believer. The term comes from the *rites of sacramental*, which are the matter and form for sacraments of the church. These customs are unlimited, and new ones continue to develop throughout time, but the church for a fuller understanding of each has categorized them: public prayer (*orens),* holy waters and oils *(tinctus),* the eating of holy or blessed food *(edens),* the general confession of sins as in the public prayers of the church at Mass, in the Divine Office and at other times *(confessus),* and charitable giving *(dans),* and blessings of devotional items by the pope and the bishops for the edification of the faithful such as ashes, palms, and candles (*benidicens).* Various degrees of indulgences have been attached to each sacramental of the church.

sacrarum also known as the *piscina*. The sink-like device that is funneled directly into the ground below the upper levels of soil so that any of the unused Precious Blood could be returned to the earth.

sacristan the lay official in charge of the sacristy of cathedrals, churches, and shrines and in monasteries and abbeys, the serving brother that fulfills the same function there.

sacristy the space set aside for the clergy to vest before sacred liturgies. In large cathedrals and basilicas this space is often separate, sometimes in a large adjoining building as in the case of the sacristy at the Vatican Basilica, which was erected close to the site where St. Peter was actually crucified.

sagrato the Italian term for Church plaza, in particular the title used at the Vatican for the part of Saint Peter's Square where the stone steps lead up to the front of the basilica. This patio-like area, including the steps, where the pope celebrates outdoor Masses officially bears the title *sagrato Vaticano*. The term sagrato also applies to a small plaza in front of any parish churches.

sakkos the dalmatic-like outer vestment of the Eastern Rite Catholic and the Orthodox churches.

Sanctitas the Latin title, meaning holiness, first used in the late sixth century for bishops but after the eight century reserved exclusively for the Roman Pontiff. From it we have the modern forms of address for popes: 'Your Holiness, His Holiness, Beatissimus Pater, Santissimo Padre and Holy Father.' For some time all of the greater patriarchs also made use of this title as did some of the lay princes of high standing. It was not until the eighteenth century that non-Christian sects began to apply this purely Latin title to their leaders.

sanctuary the area of the *chancel* in a church or cathedral where the Sacrifice of the Mass is celebrated. Also the term used in canon and civil law to identify the longstanding custom of offering safe haven to anyone seeking refuge inside a church, including those wanted for crimes.

Sanctus the conclusion of the Angelic Hymn of the choirs of angels at Bethlehem ending with the words: "Sanctus, Sanctus, Sanctus, Dominus Deus Sabaoth" which translates to "Holy, Holy, Holy Lord God of Hosts." When sung in Latin, the term Sabaoth, for Hosts, is the only Hebrew word found within the liturgy. The Sanctus came into the Mass early fifth century.

Sarum Rite See: *Rites of the Church.*

Saturday, Holy the opening of the Easter liturgy, the Vigil Mass contains the blessing of the Easter Fire, the blessing of the Easter (Paschal) candle, and other elements sanctifying the church including the baptism rite of converts. The Holy Saturday Vigil Mass is also typically the longest liturgy in the Catholic calendar.

Saturnalia the name of the pagan feast on 25 December, the winter solstice in the old calendar, dedicated to the pagan god, Saturn. It was celebrated in both England and Continental Europe, including Scandinavia, until Christianity firmly took hold around the fifth century. Saturn was the god of winter and to appease him, hoping to be spared a violent and bitter winter period, the people honored him annually on the day of the solstice by celebrating with lights (candles), delicacies, and gift giving. Children received dolls and homemade musical instruments and adults exchanged scented and painted candles.

Since the Bible did not cite the exact day of Christ's birth, the popes of the Middle Ages determined that the ecclesiastical calendar should usurp the pagan holiday of *Saturnalia* for the solemnity of Christ's birth. It encouraged the existing customs of celebrating with light, food, and gift giving but added both the birth narrative and the Holy Mass to exisiting secular customs. Along with tribal use of evergreens, mistletoe and other non-Christian rituals, the Church converted the existing seasonal traditions, incorporating them into Christian symbolism. Because the Holy Mass became the central event of the celebration, the 25 December was renamed in Old English "Christmas" which means simply "Christ's Mass."

Scala Sancta or, in English, the Holy Stairs, consisting of twenty-eight steps taken from the former palace of Pontius Pilate in Jerusalem by the Empress Helena and reconstructed first at the Lateran Palace and later transferred to a building constructed just to house them across the basilica square. Considered to be sanctified by Christ as he climbed these marble steps to the balcony of Pilate's throne room where the final judgment took place and where the Holy Week events began, today thousands of pilgrims climb them on their knees each year to receive the plenary indulgence granted (under normal terms) to those that do so piously. As such, it is one of the most popular holy sites in Rome during Holy Week.

scapular, devotional technically known as the 'scapular medals' even though they are not all made of metallic material, the sacramental of the church used to heighten the devotion of the faithful by imitating the smaller version of the habitual scapular. At the present time, the Holy See recognizes eighteen scapular devotions, most attached to one religious community or another or to one of the approved archconfraternities. After 1910, the Holy See mandated the optional use of a true medal that bore several images symbolic of the various scapular devotions already approved.

The cloth sacramental devotions comprise two large square segments of wool measuring approximately 2 inches by 2 ¼ inches upon which appear the images of that particular devotion. Threads of similar color and material connect the two segments so that the head may pass easily between them. The color of the woven wool used in each devotion mimics the original religious habit of the order that sponsors the devotion. One must be formally invested in a ceremony of blessing before the fruits of these devotions may be realized. A great many indulgences have been attached to the wearing of these sacramental scapulars.

The more famous of the these ancient cloth sacramentals are the scapulars of: Our Lady of Mount Carmel (the Brown Scapular), of Our Lady of Seven Dolors (the Black Scapular), of the Immaculate Conception (also a Black Scapular), of the Passion of Christ (also black), of the Most Precious Blood (the Red Scapular), of the Red Scapular of the Passion, of Our Lady of Bon Secours (black with a red cloth cross), of the Immaculate

Heart of Mary (white), of Saint Michael the Archangel (in the shape of a military shield, one black, one blue), of Saint Benedict (black), of Our Lady of Good Councel (white), of Saint Joseph (gold), of the Sacred Hearts of Jesus and Mary (white), of Saint Dominic (cream), of the Blue Scapular of the Immaculate Conception, of Our Lady of Ransom (white), and the Most Blessed Trinity (white with a cross worked in blue and red). There is also a special scapular of multiple devotion known as the *Five Scapulars.* This sacramental combines the five most universal devotions onto one medal or cloth devotion. For this to have efficacy, the wearer must be formally invested in all five scapulars. These are: the Red Scapular of the Passion, the Scapular of the Immaculate Conception, the Scapular of Our Lady of Mount Carmel, the Scapular of the Seven Dolors, and the Scapular of the Most Blessed Trinity.

scapular, habitual in regards to religious garb, the part of the habit of some orders of men and women religious that drapes over the shoulders in both front and back (thus its name in Latin, *scapula,* meaning the shoulder blade). It is approximately fourteen to eighteen inches wide but does not reach to the floor in front or back and is made of both the same material and color as the habit proper or of a contrasting material. The habit scapular is the source of the symbolic devotional sacramental by the same name. Originally it was called the *crux,* for cross, which it represents. It also was known by the names *jugum Christi* (yoke of Christ) and *scutum Christi* (shield of Christ). Not all religious habits made use of the scapular but nearly all the monastic orders, the post-monastic orders, the mendicants and the Renaissance era foundations of religious men and women did so. Also, many of the religious orders of women founded after 1800 likewise adopted it, as well, for their habits because of the symbolism that it represented.

schism a formal and sometimes irrevocable rupture within the church due to political unrest or grave theological differences. The term comes to us from the Greek, *schisma,* meaning to rent asunder or to divide.

Schism, Eastern an open revolt led by the Emperor of the Eastern Roman Empire based at Constantinople (where the greatest power then resided) attempting to elevate the Patriarch of Constantinople above the Bishop of Rome (i.e. Pope). This initial political quarrel fell into further division when the Byzantine clergy joined the cause to supplant Rome's authority in favor of Constantinople. Once this happened, numerous theological disputes arose which in time ended with a total breech between the Catholic Church of the East and the West. As a consequence, the East assumed the name Orthodox Church (meaning the true church) and the West remained Catholic (Universal) but added the distinction of 'Roman" to the title to affirm the ecclesial clay of papal infallibility. The title of Eastern Schism also applies to many further schisms within the Orthodox family that continued to occur for nine centuries after the breech with Rome.

Schism, the Great Western the title of the greatest, but short-lived, divide that came upon the Church of Rome in 1378 at the death of Pope Gregory XI who had resided mainly at Avignon but for the last three years of his life had returned the papacy to Rome. These three years were most dangerous as Rome was then rife with crime, and brigands and marauders roamed through the city day and night murdering anyone they came upon. So when Gregory XI died, great unease spread throughout the church as many of the political and ecclesial authorities of that time had interests in remaining in the Eternal City even though the decay of the city warranted a return to more peaceful Avignon.

Within rapid succession a pope was elected at both Rome and Avignon with Europe divided in loyalty between the two for more than twenty years. In 1409 the church convened a council at Pisa to resolve the dispute but rather than do so, in the election of yet another pope, a third division arose as the first two popes refused to abdicate. After 1409 papal regimes now existed concurrently at Rome, Pisa, and at Avignon. At first, the new candidate gained most adherents with Avignon loosing the most territory to the Pisan claimant. But Rome seemed to most to be the legitimate pontiff, despite the fewest initial adherents, as in short order the Pisan candidate (who reigned as John XXIII) behaved so disgracefully that all that initially adhered to his cause abandoned him (and because of his behavior, no pope again took the name John until 1958). The weakened Avignon candidate was likewise thereafter referred to as an *anti-pope* despite continued claims to legitimacy.

This schism continued to divide Europe (thus the title of Great Western Schism) until 1417 when the Council of Constance imposed the abdications of all three existing claimants to the papacy, and elected a candidate acceptable to all factions, who took the name Martin V (1417-1431) and the permanently return of the papacy to the See of Rome.

seal the legal emblem of a canonical jurisdiction of the church, which is fixed to all ecclesial and/or civil legal documents issued by these jurisdictions according to the terms of both church and local civil law. The formal emblem of a person of rank/office within the Church all of which are governed by the ecclesiastical rubrics of heraldry. *See also: Heraldry in the Catholic Church.*

Secret Sacrament the term once used to refer to the Sacrament of Penance because it was administered entirely in the dark secrecy of the confessional. Today, following the adaptations made to the Sacrament of Penance, especially the inclusion of face-to-face confession, this term is seldom applied by clerics and never so by liturgists.

seculars diocesan priests; priests that do not belong to one of the religious orders or communities but that are incardinated to a specific diocese. Also known today as 'diocesan priests.'

sedia gestatoria the portable throne used to carry the popes aloft in processions in and around Rome for centuries. It was intended more to elevate the office of the papacy, creating an aura of regal mystery, than as a means to relieve a pope from the stress of strenuous ceremonies. Retired by John Paul II in 1978 it has since been replaced by a rolling pedestal on which the current pope can either stand erect or be seated on a mobile throne.

sedilia technically the term for the south side of the chancel and where the clergy were always seated until the second half of the twentieth century. For this reason, the clerical pew where the clergy sat came to bear this same name. Typically, a sedilia is made of expensive hard wood, is ornamental in design, and seat three or four persons. In Gothic architecture these seats were often made of stone and imbedded into the southern wall of the sanctuary. Often times, either in stone or wood, ornate canopies hung overhead. A portable form of the sedilia continues in use today for concelebrants in cathedrals.

See a term for diocese or archdiocese from the Latin, *sede,* meaning a 'seat' in reference to the throne, or cathedra, used by the bishop within his jurisdiction and from which his authority stems. Although each diocese is also simultaneously a See, the church applies this term most commonly to the Holy See, or Apostolic See, two terms referring to the Universal Church governed by the Roman Pontiff.

Servant of God the title that the church bestows upon a person whose cause for sainthood has officially been opened and thus the first step in the formal cause for canonization. At the moment, perhaps the most famous Servant of God is Pope John Paul II. The title is always used when writing or speaking the name of the deceased and may be used either prior, to or immediately after, the name. For example this title may appear either as *'Servant of God, John Paul II'* or as *'John Paul II, Servant of God'*.

Servant of the Servants of God one of the titles still utilized by the popes in the litany of offices embodied in the Petrine Office. In Latin it is rendered as *Servus Servorum Dei* as first utilized by Pope Saint Gregory the Great (A.D. 590-604) as a result of a conflict between the Patriarch of Constantinople and the Bishop of Rome in which the patriarch claimed superiority to the pope. To counter his argument, Pope Gregory reacted by assuming humility rather than superiority and thus created for himself this title. Few of his successors in the papacy accepted this title until the late ninth century when it appeared from time to time until the middle twelfth century. This title returned to the papacy fully after the closing of the Second Vatican Council (1965) and remains one of the more important, following that of 'Bishop of Rome,' as a consequence of a change in the formal persona of the Petrine Office.

seven the number of the greatest significance in Old Testament theology. Every seven days is declared the Sabbath, every seven month is declared sacred and every seventh year is set aside for rest and spiritual renewal thus the modern tern 'sabbatical year'. The great Hebrew Jubilee Years were set at an interval of every forty-nines years-seven years time seven and several feasts lasted seven days each. In the Christian liturgical calendar, the feast of Pentecost occurs seven times seven days after the Easter event. Much of this numerology entered the Christian church as well but in the fourth century, the celebration of an eight day began in certain Christian holidays (See: *Octave).*

sexton a person hired by the pastor to care for the physical plant of the parish complex.

shamiana an alternate term for the baldachin or baldachino coming into English from Indo-Hindu culture.

shofar the horn of any animal other than the cow or calf but preferably from the adult ram used to close the fast at Yom Kippur and at other times such as during Rosh Hashanah in the Jewish religion but likewise considered a part of the final coming of Christ on earth, which Scripture says will be known by its mournful call.

sign of the Cross the most important of the church's sacramentals because it is the common sign of all believer's deliverance from sinfulness, evil, and from Satan's influence. It is also the sign of our common faith, and the emblem of God's mercy as manifested in the person of His only Son, Jesus Christ on the Cross of Calvary. The sign of the Cross is also the affirmation of all believers in the Triune God and in the Incarnation, Death and Resurrection of Savior. The sign of the Cross came into the Church in the Middle Ages where it had already been adopted socially as a form of greeting to passers-by. This social custom entered the modern era during the Apostolic Age when the Apostles and earliest followers of Christ used the marking of the forehead, lips and breast as a secret way of greeting fellow Christians. This special mode of marking oneself with the sign of the Cross, has remained in the Church for two thousand years and is now the proper mode of marking oneself at the opening words of the Gospel.

Silence, grand the period between the end of night prayers and the opening of morning prayer in monasteries when total silence is observed.

The custom originated in the middle third century and became a part of the monastic rule of many orders by the eighth century.

Societies, Apostolic Life a form of religious institute where members do not take formal vows and where each members can be moved to any house within the institute's organization. They are permitted to serve within the diocese that welcomes them but they remain technically a part of their institute rather than a part of the diocesan clergy of that place. Examples of some of the religious communities that fall into this category of religious life are the Maryknoll Fathers, the various groups of Oratorians, the Sulpician Fathers, and the Vincentians (also known as the Lazarist Fathers). Typically, these groups live within society, moving freely amongst those whom them serve.

societies, pious similar to confraternities and archconfraternities but which have not been canonically erected and thus do not enjoy protection of the Holy See or another competent canonical authority, these groups sprang up in times of spiritual need for the purpose of conducting good works and for promoting pious activity. Some of these groups maintain a costume or uniform while others never assumed such. Examples of the most well known of these modern pious societies are the Society for the Propagation of the Faith, the Society of the Holy Family, the Saint Vincent de Paul Society, the League of the Sacred Heart, the Legion of Mary and the Knights of Columbus which is, in reality, neither a papal order or a confraternity of the church.

sodality a form of pious society or confraternity.

Solidarnosc the title, in original Polish, of the Solidarity Movement that swept across Poland in the early 1980s, its success due in large measure to the open support of Pope John Paul II and his papacy, which led in due course to not only the overthrow of the Communist regime in Poland but to the fall of Communism throughout Europe. Headed by union activist (and later Polish State President) Lech Walesa the Solidarity Movement was reinforced by the late pope, Ronald Reagan and the United States government and by Margaret Thatcher and the government of the United Kingdom.

spire a single tower in church architecture usually concealing a church bell, almost always ornate in design.

Spy Wednesday the title applied to the Wednesday of Holy Week, but seldom used since Vatican Council II, commemorating the traitorous act of Judas Iscariot who agreed on the day before the Last Supper to hand Christ over to the authorities (on what would become known as Good Friday) for the price of forty pieces of silver.

Stabat Mater a hymn employed in the church that tells of the sorrows of the Blessed Virgin at the foot of the Cross of Calvary. It was written by don Giacopone da Todi in 1306 and soon after came into usage throughout the Universal Church. It is one of the more somber sequences in Catholic hymnody.

standard, heraldic a flag made up entirely of the heraldic achievement of an individual or noble/royal house. It may be flown on a flagstaff or on a car or may be displayed in other ways. The standard, like the personal coat of arms, immediately identifies the bearer as the heraldic design upon it is unique in every way. The heraldic standard is also the privilege traditionally granted to nobleman and others that have the right to bear a coat of arms in place of the white funereal pall. There are two ways to display a heraldic standard. The first depicts the entire heraldic achievement in miniature upon a white field or banner. In this style, the arms appear in the center of the cloth of the flag. This style is known as the Continental style as it is preferred in continental Europe. The second form of standard manufacture is known as the British style. In this form, the elements found within the border of the shield of a coat of arms extend to all the borders of the cloth so that the entire banner is covered by heraldic emblems.

Stational churches a practice unique to Rome. In the Lenten Season forty historic churches are visited, one on each of the days of Lent, where the Mass is celebrated and devotions offered. Often times, pilgrims undertaking this forty-day pilgrimage walk in common procession to the assigned church each day. As the ritual of visiting these churches is specified in advance and follows a time-honored custom, groups from different nations visit them on the same day but at different hours. Thus the *Stational Church* Lenten pilgrimage can be embraced at numerous times throughout each of the forty days of Lent. The Church long ago assigned indulgences to those able to undertake this Lenten pilgrimage.

Stationary, proper forms and use of Churchmen and laity alike should make use of proper forms of stationary for both formal and everyday use. The rank or office of a cleric determines what is proper in terms of color and design (see chapter on protocol). The laity, however should also make use of dignified personal stationary, something many in the computerized age fail to recognize.

The most formal type of stationary is the *engraved* form. In this form, the paper used is pressed against an etched copper plate containing the name or image desired. The result provides a slightly raised luxurious effect, which may be rendered without inks, thus known as *blind embossing*, or it may be dusted by ink to provide color. The next formal method of creating stationary is known properly as the *letterpress* style, which is a slightly indented form, again using a custom plate to produce the lettering or image desired. This is the style of printing used for the first edition of the Gutenberg Bible. *Thermography* is the third, and less formal, style. It is created by placing hot resin atop a flat image or lettering, which rises higher than other printed forms once cooled. Finally, the use of *offset lithography* may be used as this style lays flat, one color, letters or images upon the page by use of a roller vs. an engraved plate.

When producing quality stationary, one should also include the tissue lining inside the envelope, which the most formal mode calls for. As such, cardinals should use red tissue, patriarchs, archbishops and bishops, green and black for the monsignori, priests and deacons. Laymen and women may use the color of preference for the tissue lining, but the most dignified remain the more muted colors or white.

For mourning periods, black is used as a lining for a period of six months, followed by deep gray for the remainder of the first year for those that wish to observe this custom. Sometimes mauve or purple are used after the period set aside for gray or in place of it altogether. During mourning periods, a thin border of black or gray is also sometimes used to edge the papers and envelope.

steps, altar it is customary for there to be an uneven number of steps on the platform supporting the altar of sacrifice. In the first century there were no steps at all, the altar resting on the floor. Between the second and eight centuries three steps were customary. In the Gothic and later Baroque periods, where the cathedrals were grander, seven steps became typical so that the altar would be high enough to be seen throughout the long nave.

stipends a priest or bishop is entitled to receive an honorarium for the role that they play in the celebration of the Mass and other sacraments. The acceptance of a stipend carries the burden of completing the intention of the petitioner. For instance, a priest may accept a token sum as a stipend to celebrate a Mass for the soul of a beloved family member but that priest is required under penalty of sin to do so in a timely fashion. This custom came into use at a time when the clergy earned no salary of any kind. As such these small honoraria permitted them to function in a society requiring some access to money. In some places this custom became corrupt but by and large, the custom of minimal stipends is a good one and has served the church well.

stole, altar a long, narrow cloth typically of ornate or rich material that is draped over the altar from side to side so that the terminus at either side fall down the sides of the altar, ending in a spade, or pointed shape—sometimes employing tassels or other decorative devices. Although most popular since the second half of the twentieth century, the altar stole actually was first used in the second century.

style properly referred to as a 'style of office,' the term applied to the qualification that accompanies a formal religious, royal, or state title of an individual of high rank. A style is more or less the proper form of address for persons of rank such as "His/Your Holiness" for a pope, "His/Your Eminence" for a cardinal, or "His/Your Excellency" for bishops and archbishops. In royal terms, styles are most commonly "His/Her/Your Majesty", His/Her/Your Royal Highness", and "His/Her/Your Serene Highness."

sua sponte is the Italian counterpart for the phrase or term, *motu proprio,* meaning by the pope's own initiative. The latter term is applied when a reigning pope wishes to issue a decree without consulting his cardinals or the Roman Curia. The Italian equivalent, *sua sponte,* is not used by the Catholic Church but it has come into secular use in various nations' courts of law. In these instances, the phrase translates to 'by the personal motion of the sitting judge or justice' and comes into play when the court desires to pronounce a ruling without any prompting from either party with business before the court. On rare occasions, the term *sua sponte* is used by the heads of one or another of the numerous Protestant sects for the same canonical reasons so that they are not accused of being 'Roman' by use of the more historic papal phrase *motu proprio.*

sub-deacon one of the now extinct offices in Minor Orders. This rank came into the church in the third century, intended as assistants to the deacons. Their role in the liturgy originally resembled that of the modern 'altar server' but in the seventh century they were also permitted to read the Epistles at Masses celebrated by bishops. Before Vatican II, this office was the first requiring total celibacy within Holy Orders.

Subha although it resembles the Holy Rosary, and is often incorrectly mistaken for it, this is the title of the wooden prayer beads used by Muslims.

Suburbicarian See, papal decree a *motu proprio* decree entitled "**Suburbicariis sedibus**" issued by Pope John XXIII on April 11, 1962 and which established a rule that the cardinal bishops of the church would no longer have ordinary jurisdiction over the suburbicarian sees surrounding Rome which had been entrusted to them as members of the College of Cardinal-Bishops. After this decree, these dioceses were to be thereafter ruled by bishops with complete and independent ordinary power, that is to say legates in the Cardinal-Bishop's names but with full powers to govern.

Cardinal bishops would thereafter only retain the title of the see, not the actual right to govern. Wishing to make a permanent change in the law, Pope John XXIII did not permit those already in office to loose the rights to govern the suburbicarian sees previously entrusted to them. Those that retained these rights after the changes made by John XXIII were Cardinals Eugene Tisserant, Benedetto Aloisi Masella and Giuseppe Pizzardo.

sudarium the white linen napkin that was attached to the crozier of Latin Rite bishops, abbots and abbesses until the beginning of the twentieth century. It came into use in the early eleventh century, intended to absorb the moister on the ungloved hand of the bishop. Originally it was simply knotted onto the staff but soon became attached with fanciful cords. By the twelfth century it was commonly made of silk or cambric and measured sixty-four (64) by sixteen (16) inches. Because of the larger size, most of this cloth would hang low onto the crozier and so it became the custom in the fourteenth century to twist it around the staff several times. The sudarium has not been used by bishops for many generations but continues in the usage of abbots and abbesses although this is almost entirely relegated in the twenty-first century to the heraldic renderings of this staff of office for these persons.

sui juris or in proper ecclesial Latin, *sui iuris*, meaning 'of or pertaining to an autonomous church' (within the Catholic Church). Each of the major rites of the church, including the Latin Rite, is *sui juris* in jurisdiction. The church also uses this designation for smaller canonical jurisdictions that do not have sufficient number of parishes or clergy to be elevated to the status of diocese or for that matter to the status of prefecture apostolic or vicariate apostolic.

summus episcopus although a Latin title loosely translating to 'chief bishop' one must not presume this office to be Roman Catholic. In fact, it is the title granted to the head of the Evangelical Lutheran Church in Prussia by King Frederick William III in 1798, who as monarch became the *de jure* leader of the Protestant movement in his lands and thus the first incumbent in this office. Frederick William had been born a Prussian Lutheran but converted before his ascension to the throne to the Calvinist (Reformed) Church. Upon becoming king, not wishing to offend the majority of his Lutheran subjects, he ordered the merger of the two distinct Protestant churches within his realm thus creating Evangelical Lutheranism.

superior the title granted to senior officials within religious orders (both male and female), sometimes to designate the head of a convent or monastery, sometimes to refer to regional officers entrusted with more wide ranging powers.

supreme bishop a strictly Protestant term that arose in the Post-Reformation monarchies in northern Europe intended to imitate the role of the Supreme Pontiff of the Holy Roman Church viz a vis ecclesial power, jurisdiction, and supremacy. Initially this title was applied to preeminent clerics in the Lutheran, Evangelical Protestant, or Calvinistic churches but it fell away by the 18th century everywhere but within the Kingdom of Prussia. At Berlin, the supreme bishop of the Prussian Union (the official Lutheran Church in northern Germany) vested this post in the person of the King of Prussia (and later simultaneously in him as Emperor of Germany) as *ex officio* head of the German Protestant church. This role remained a great source of irritation between German Catholics and Protestants through the 1930s.

Swiss Guard, Pontifical See separate chapter on this subject

synod a formal, canonical gathering of churchmen and approved laity under the authority of the church to discuss serious matters. A diocesan synod concerns itself with local church matters under the presidency of the local bishop which the Synod of Bishops, seated at Rome, assembles the College of Bishops (either for the Universal Church or for the church by regions or by common language) to discuss matters of concern for the entire church or for those specific regions.

tabernacle an ornate repository reserved for the Blessed Sacrament, sometimes also referred to as an *ostensorium* and as a *ciborium*. Also the title for the stone crypt used to house a saint's relic inside a fixed altar.

Tau crozier the pastoral staff used by the Byzantine bishops took the shape of the Tau cross in place of the crook of a shepherd as in the Latin Rite in the eleventh century. In short order the terminus of the two arms of the Tau became more elaborate, with serpents taking the place of other forms of terminus by the twelfth century. Many symbolic meanings have been attached to the use of serpents in the Byzantine hierarchy staffs but the most ancient of these is that the twisting serpents were intended to represent the virtue of prudence. The Tau crozier of the Byzantines is also much shorter than the crozier used by bishops in the West and unlike the Latin bishops, is carried rather than utilized as a elongated walking stick.

Te Deum the most loved hymn of Thanksgiving of the Church, the title deriving from the first few Latin words of the ritual, *Te Deum laudamus,* meaning "we give praise to Thee, O Lord" and believed to be written my Saint Ambrose of Milan (and thus also known as the *Ambrosian Hymn).* This ancient hymn originated in mid-fifth century. Very formal European liturgies, especially state and royal occasions, are most commonly referred to as the TE DEUM rather than as a Mass because the

Te Deum prayer ritual is always recited at the conclusion of these very solemn pontifical Masses. The equivalent in English speaking countries would be the Mass of Thanksgiving. It was the Te Deum that was sung by those honored to be present at the deathbed of Pope John Paul II as a way of praising God for the gift of this great man.

Tenebrae the solemn liturgy of the word marked by the lighting and somber distinguishing of the candelabra by the same name, celebrated on Good Friday afternoon.

Terra Sancti Benedicti meaning 'in the land of Saint Benedict' is the canonical term for the territory near to the abbey of Montecassino given over to the Benedictine order as a *seignory* (lay lordship) by Pope Victor II in AD 1057. It had come into the hands of the papacy in AD 744 in the testament of Gisulf II of Benevento. Once given over, the territory was administered by the abbot bringing great wealth to Montecassino and the Benedictine order. In time it grew to include the principalities of Benevento and that of Pontecorvo. Today these lands no longer carry civil administration nor ownership by the abbey but the abbot of Montecassino does still govern all of these territories as *abbot nullius* therefore making it an ecclesial community directly subject to the Holy See.

territorium proprium a Latin phrase used by Rome for the Oriental churches so that when an Oriental priest is raised to the hierarchy with much of his new flock being spread throughout the world, thus living outside the *proper territory*, it is said that his jurisdiction includes those living outside the *territorium proprium.*

tertiaries lay persons of either sex living according to the rule of life of one of the religious orders such as the Benedictines, Dominicans, or Augustinians. Tertiaries do not live in community nor do they adopt a distinct for of garb but they do enjoy the privilege of being buried in the habit of the order to which they have become attached.

tibularum (sometimes referred to as *tibulum*) the Roman (classical Latin) term for the heavy wooden crossbar, or transverse arm, of the crosses used for the act of crucifixion, the capital punishment for non-Roman citizens in the empire. The tibularum would typically weigh twice the weight of the average man who would be forced to carry it across his back and neck from the place of judgment to the site of crucifixion.

tippet a stole-like vestment used in the Church of England (and by some of the clergy in churches that sprang forth from it) worn exclusively for Evening Prayer or Vespers. It is worn about the neck, is often black in color, and bears ecclesiastical images or monograms. The tippet is not interchangeable with the stole in these churches, which is always worn at formal liturgies.

titular archiepiscopal sees those titles of former or suppresses Sees that were equal to the rank and office of archbishop/archbishopric and which are now awarded to titular archbishops. Presently there are eighty-eight such sees which combined with the titular metropolitan sees are conferred upon non-residential archbishops.

titular episcopal sees those titles of former or suppressed Sees that were equal to the dioceses or bishoprics of today and which are now awarded to all titular bishops. Presently there are one thousand-eight hundred and seventy-nine established titular sees for non-residential bishops.

titular metropolitan sees those titles of former or suppressed Sees that were equal to the rank and office of today's metropolitan sees and which are awarded as such to the highest class of titular archbishops. Presently there are ninety-five such Sees in use.

tonsure a mark of membership in the clerical state. Tonsure in religious orders and amongst the mendicants included the full shaving of the crown of the head. Tonsure for the congregations and modern societies, as well as the secular clergy after the Renaissance, was limited to the symbolic shaving of a small amount of hair near the rear of the head but these customs were laid aside for the most part after the Second Vatican Council in 1965. Tonsure is also the name of one of the offices in *Minor Orders* prior to 1965. There were different forms of tonsure.

The secular, or diocesan, clerics came to wear only the symbolic tonsure by the fifteen hundreds. As seen, this comprised a small cut of the hair behind the ear near to the crown of the head and thus mainly unnoticeable. The various religious orders preferred to mandate a style unique to their own orders and the church in various regions likewise developed styles of their own. For instance, the *coronal tonsure,* or the *tonsure of Saint Peter,* required a completely shaved crown of the head so that entire top of the cleric's head was bald was in use in England, Spain, Portugal and Italy as early as the second century. The *Eastern tonsure* or Greek tonsure also took the name of the *tonsure of Saint Paul* and required the cleric to shave the entire head. The *tonsure of Saint James,* or the Scottish tonsure, required shaving just the front of the head so that from ear to ear up and across the head the forehead and hair behind it was completely shorn. Great ceremonies, in the cathedrals during ordinations and in abbeys during reception of new members, were attached to the rite of the tonsure.

tower façade a church façade that includes at least two towers at the front of the building. This style was most common in American church architecture after the late 1870s lasting and until the post-Vatican II period. Nearly every North American diocese can, in fact, point to fine examples of this style church within their own borders. Sometimes it is also referred to as "American Neo-Gothic" or "American Neo-Romanesque" style.

tracery the English language term for the fretted and elegant stone work that frames the elaborate stained glass windows in Europe's greatest cathedrals and churches. This term is likewise applied to the interior support designs within the windows as well.

transept the transverse arm (aisle) of a cruciform church.

transient parish an English language term applied to a cathedral that simultaneously stands as a canonical parish. This is the general norm in North America but elsewhere a cathedral remains outside the parish structure remaining the seat of the bishop of the place and open to all. The term *transient parish* alerts Catholics that cathedral is both the seat of the bishop and simultaneously a parish of the diocese but one that is open to all for worship and receipt of the sacraments.

Triregno the Italian term for the Triple Crown or papal tiara. In Latin the official title is *triregnum because* this state headdress comprises a full beehive shaped bonnet on which are affixed three ornate diadems or crowns. It is the simply of the pope as supreme pontiff of the universal church. In the earliest days of the papacy, the popes wore the *phrygium,* which comprised a stiffened white cap and veil. By the ninth century, this soft cap took a stiffened form and was mounted with a golden diadem. This began the period of the papal monarchy and the vesture of the popes soon developed in recognition of it. By the thirteenth century, the cloth was stiffened and assumed great height similar to those of the twentieth century and the diadem at its base took on the alternating key patter (like the top of a castle wall) and became more richly ornamented. At this time, the infulæ (properly called the *caudæ* when referring to those appearing on the papal tiara) first appeared, clearly stemming from the mitre design. Oddly, these were worked in black cloth until the late fifteenth century. During the pontificate of Boniface VIII (1294-1303) the second diadem appeared. The third diadem appeared for the first time in 1316 during the reign of John XXII (1316-1334) at the time that the papacy resided at Avignon.

True Cross found in Jerusalem by the Empress Helena in the fourth century, the earliest Christians preserved the Cross on which Christ was crucified and secretly venerated by the young Church. Helena afterwards returned to Rome with it and other precious relics associated with Christ's Passion. Known thereafter as the *True Cross,* it has been dismantled through the ages to create relics. Some of these are very large but most were reduced to splinters and have been included ever since in the pectoral crosses worn by bishops.

tunica alba the ancient Greek garment from which is derived the liturgical alb.

tunicle the dalmatic-like vestment worn by the office of sub-deacon (now defunct) and by bishops prior to 1965. Prior to this time, bishops donned the alb, stole, tunicle, dalmatic and chasuble when celebrating the Sacred Liturgy. When used by sub-deacons, the garb matched the vestments of the priest celebrating the Mass but were much more light weight in form. The tunicle is still used by those granted the indult to celebrate the Tridentine Mass but not by other clerics in the Catholic Church.

Twelve Days of Christmas the period each year between December 25 and January 6, the Feast of the Epiphany of Our Lord, in which the season of Christmas is celebrated widely throughout the Christian world (although liturgically speaking the Christmas season in the church extends from Christmas Eve through to the feast of the Baptism of the Lord on the second Sunday in January).

Twelve Days of Christmas A Christmas carol of secret Catholic symbolic richness. Immediately following Henry VIII's break with the Church of Rome, Catholics throughout the British Isles were barred from practicing their faith in public; to do so carried with it a sentence of death. From 1558 until 1829 when laws were amended that once again permitted safe public worship by Catholics, one had to be a secret member of the church and so devout British Catholics needed to find ways to celebrate their Catholic faith while at the same time disguising this celebration from the authorities. As such hymns, carols, and prayers were often disguised as seasonal poems or popular songs, the words having a double meaning, one religious known only to Catholics and the other secular and sung by all.

One of the most famous English Catholic Christmas carols (believed to be nothing more than a holiday secular canticle, was in fact written by secret Catholics as a celebration of their faith, unbeknownst to government officials or Anglicans throughout England— *The Twelve Days of Christmas.*

All of the gifts provided on each of the twelve days had a secret religious symbolism intended for British Catholics alone: The *partridge in a pear tree* presented Jesus Christ. The *two turtle doves* on the second day were symbolic of the Old and New Testaments. The third day's *three French hens* stood for faith hope and love while the fourth day's *four calling birds* represented the four Gospels in Sacred Scripture (the works of the Evangelists Matthew, Mark, Luke & John). The *five golden rings* given on day five call to mind the Torah, the formal title for the first five books of the Old Testament while s*ix geese a-laying* stood for the six days that it took for God to create the earth as He wished. *Seven swans a-swimming* represented the seven blessed gifts of the Holy Spirit (Prophesy, Service, Teaching, Exhortation, Contribution, Leadership, and Mercy). On day eight the gifts presented were *eight maids a-milking* representing the Eight Beatitudes presented by Christ on the Mount. *Nine ladies dancing* are symbolic of the nine fruits of the Holy Spirit (Charity, Joy, Peace, Patience, Kindness, Goodness, Fidelity, Gentleness, and Self Control). The Ten Commandments are represented in the carol by *ten lords a-leaping* while *eleven pipers piping* represented the eleven remaining apostles (those remaining faithful to Christ after Judas' betrayal). Finally, the authors used the *twelve drummers drumming* to symbolize the twelve main dogmas embraced in the Apostles' Creed, a foundation of Catholic belief. Of course, the giver of these gifts in the carol, identified as "My true Love" is God Himself whose ultimate gift to mankind was His only Son.

U

umbellam the Latin title for canopy including its usage as a fixed canopy above an altar and as the clothe canopy used to protect the Blessed Sacrament in procession. *See: Baldachino.*

usus rochetti the title of the papal indult that permits the use of the rochet, the prelatial outer garb resembling the surplice, to those groups not normally invested with the prelatial dignity and thus not normally entitled to wear it. Because of a secondary role that they play in the church, however, these special groups may also have occasional use to wear the rochet and as such the Holy See has provided an indult for them so to do. Such groups would be the various chapters of canons throughout the world and the knight-members and the priest-chaplains of the Equestrian Order of the Holy Sepulchre of Jerusalem and the Knights of Malta (only when vesting in the mozzetta specific to these two orders). In all of these cases, the use of ecclesial lace in the design and the incorporation of amaranth red silk at the sleeves are granted.

utroque iure a Latin title translating to 'both laws' in reference to a doctoral degree awarded in both canon and civil law as a joint degree. This specific, simultaneous dual degree is awarded in pontifical universities in Italy primarily, but is also still awarded by some Italian civil universities as a carryover from an era when these universities were governed by the Papal States. The *utroque iure* degree can likewise be earned on the licentiate level.

veil the top piece of a nun's habit made of clothe and fastened to other items comprising the headdress of a religious order. Made of cloth, sometimes black, sometimes white, and gray or other colors, the *veil* entirely encompasses the head and is intended to invoke the theme of virginal modesty. Postulants to religious life wore a modified veil while novices traditionally wore a white version of the professed nun's headdress. But modern habits have either abandoned the *veil* altogether or have shortened it considerably. A veil also forms a part of the headdress of some priests in the Byzantine Rites as well as those for the prelates of the Orthodox churches.

veil, humeral a large rectangular cloth made of a material and color similar to the *cope* closed with an ornate clasp and used over the vestment to handle the monstrance for the veneration of the Blessed Sacrament at benediction and during the *Corpus Christi* (sometimes called *Corpus Domine*) celebrations.

Venerable Order in full, "the Grand Priory in the British Realm of the Most Venerable Order of the Hospital of Saint John of Jerusalem" and the legitimate counterpart of the Roman Catholic Sovereign Military Order of Saint John of Jerusalem, of Rhoades and of Malta (S.M.O.M) for Protestants in the British Empire. Queen Victoria founded the Venerable

Order of Saint John in 1888 under the Grand Mastership of her son, the then Prince of Wales (later Edward VII), for devout Anglicans and Protestants in an attempt to restore, with full legitimacy, the historic work of the original Catholic foundation of the order of St. John in the United Kingdom. Unlike the S.M.O.M., the Venerable Order is not sovereign and may not receive or accredit diplomatic missions.

The Knights of Malta were present in England as early as 1352 and included 120 knights by 1525 but Henry VIII abolished the order in 1539. The Catholic priory of the order in Scotland suffered the same fate under the Stuarts a decade or so later. On November 26, 1963 the chanceries of both the Roman Catholic and the Anglican orders signed a joint declaration officially recognizing the other but membership in the Sovereign Order of Saint John of Jerusalem, of Rhoades and of Malta is still restricted to practicing Roman Catholics. The Order of Merit of Malta, however, is not and the Venerable Order will today receive nominations of persons of the Roman Catholic faith.

vere nullius dioecesis the canonical term meaning *'of no diocese'* which refers to the jurisdiction of an abbot over several places near to his abbey in the same way a bishop has jurisdiction over his diocese. In the abbey nullius setting, the abbot has the full rights of a bishop both within the abbey and over the clergy and populace of the places assigned to his abbey. In some instances these territories are not even contiguous. There have never been such special ecclesial jurisdictions in North America but in Europe there have been many including those still standing today including the Abbey of Montecassino.

verger the liturgical post that leads the procession in the Anglican Church, this official always seen carrying the staff of that office and the functionary that typically escorts others to the ambo or pulpit. This post developed from that of *grand macebearer,* a papal office that no longer exists.

versus populum the Latin phrase that translates to *'facing the people'* and which refers to the orientation of the priests and bishops as they celebrate the Mass after Vatican Council II. It was long claimed that as the popes have always celebrated the Mass facing the people inside St. Peter's

Basilica that it was intended all along for the church to do so universally. Indeed, the popes have celebrated the Mass under the great baldachino in the new St. Peter's and likewise under the marble canopy that stood there in the old basilica of Constantine before it but this was because the architectural demands of the Vatican Hill made it impossible to face east while celebrating Mass there. This argument does not hold water for another reason as the popes did not consider either the old Constantinian Basilica of the Vatican or the new Saint Peter's to be their own church and seldom celebrated Mass there through the centuries. It was not until the self-enforced exile after 1870 that the Vatican became the focus of the papacy. Before this time, the Lateran maintained the place of honor for eleven centuries. Thereafter there was the move to Avignon and papal residency at the Quirinale. St. Peter's Basilica was most certainly an important shrine but it did not hold the historic role it now enjoys viz. the papacy until 1870.

vestibule the narthex or atrium of a church or the anteroom entrance of a palace or public building.

vestments the garb worn by deacons, priests and bishops during the sacred liturgy. These items have great historical import in their own right but after 1969 have been greatly simplified by the Church. Those most commonly seen at liturgies today are the *chasuble,* the cape-like mantle worn for the celebration of the Mass (appearing in the colors assigned to each individual liturgical day); the matching *stole* worn about the neck; and the *alb*, or white gown. Bishops additionally make use of the *mitre*, a conical or pointed hat symbolizing their office. The *cope* is a long cape-like vestment worn by all clerics for specific liturgies outside the Mass. The color of this garb is also tied to the liturgical calendar. Deacons wear the *dalmatic* and the stole.

vestry the place set-aside for the functionaries of the liturgy to prepare and to dress, or to *vest*, from which the place takes its name. (See: *Sacristy)*

vicars, administration the title of *Vicar for Administration* is a relatively new one, created by churchmen who wished to model diocesan administration on corporate business models. In these quasi-corporate administrations, the *Vicars for Administration* are the senior most officials of a diocese under the bishop. They should also be *vicars general* in conformance with Canon Law.

vicar apostolic the title of a prelate who governs an ecclesial territory below the status of diocese, known as a *vicariate apostolic.* A *Vicar Apostolic* may hold the personal title of bishop or archbishop, and would be referred to as such in correspondence and social discourse, but his office within the structure of the Church would be recognized as the lower rank of *Vicar Apostolic.*

vicar capitular the diocesan administrator elected by either the chapter of canons of the cathedral, if there are such in the place, or by the college of consultors in that see at the time of the death or sudden departure of the diocesan bishop. This official has the powers of the bishop in terms of administration of the place but not his episcopal authority. He remains in office only until the Holy See names the succeeding bishop. Election of the vicar capitular, or diocesan administrator as it is more commonly known in English, must take place within eight days of the vacancy of the see and the one chosen must be a priest of at least thirty-five years of age.

vicar forane a diocesan official, similar to a dean of a district.

vicar general the senior official of a diocese after the ordinary who is typically an archbishop or bishop. There may be more than one *vicar general* at one time especially when there are several auxiliary, or assistant, bishops in the place. The Code of Canon Law recognizes the right of all auxiliary bishops to be nominated as *vicars general.* The *Vicars General,* even when not titular bishops, take precedence over all the other clergy of the diocese.

The pope appoints a *vicar general for the Diocese of Rome,* always a cardinal who governs the diocese in the pope's name, and a *vicar general for the Vatican City State* who likewise governs the church for the pope in the Vatican territory. This latter position is necessary because the Vatican is both a sovereign nation independent of Italy, and thus not a part of the diocese of Rome, and an ecclesial entity in its own right known as the *Holy See.* Until the early 1990s, the post of *Vicar General for Vatican City* was always in the domain of the Order of Augustinian Hermits. They held this post, originally called the *Papal Sacristan,* for six centuries before Pope John Paul II merged it with the post of Archpriest of the Vatican Basilica of St. Peter's.

vidame from the Latin, *vicedominus,* a French title applied to high-born laymen who were appointed by an absentee bishop, abbot or abbot-nullius to govern an ecclesiastical establishment in his name in the same way a vicar general governs a diocese in the absence of the sitting bishop. This title was never abolished but has lapsed into obscurity due to its general disuse during the past three centuries. Typically, it was an 'in commendam' prelate in absentia that made use of the office of vidame.

vimp the functionary in the liturgy who carries the bishop's mitre and crozier and for this purpose wears a humeral veil-like cloth over the shoulders, which is also known as a *vimp.*

virger the title in the Church of England of the post typically assigned to a lay master of ceremonies, most notably for the purpose of marshalling processions. The title came into the Anglican Church from Rome from a time when lay nobles filled a similar position at the Lateran. The title derives from the Latin word for 'white' as the incumbent typically carried a white staff of office. Today, non-clerical offices also bear this title, most notably the office of the Lord Steward of England who receives a white staff as a mark of his office. From the Latin 'virga' is also derived the phrase 'verge of the court', to describe the area over which the Lord Steward used to have civil and criminal jurisdiction.

Vulgate the Latin term referring to the original Greek-to-Latin translation of Sacred Scripture. Greek was the scholarly language at the time that the Evangelists penned the Sacred Scriptures and as such this Greek *New Testament* is the most accurate. The first Latin edition of the original Greek, however, known as the *Vulgate,* is likewise generally considered by scholars to be accurate and is credited to the great scholar Saint Jerome who translated it.

It is to this ancient Latin text that scholars most frequently refer when seeking an accurate citation of Sacred Scripture. Sadly, each subsequent translation, including numerous modernizations introduced to keep current with linguistic and political adaptations through the ages, are not as faithful to the original Greek or to the first accurate translation into Latin, which we still continue to refer to as the *vulgate.*

warden a title found in the Catholic Church only in the British Isles, the layperson elected or appointed to assist the pastor and to care for the management of the physical complex of the parish.

Water, Holy the water of the church blessed by a priest or bishop for the use of the people as a sacramental. Water has played an important role in both the Old Testament and the New because it is the symbol of life and cleansing. The ancients used it as well to symbolize purification such as the Greeks, the Romans (as we know from Pontius Pilate), the Egyptians, and Persians. Mosaic Law requires ritual cleansing of all persons within the rituals of Judaism, of their sacred vessels, of the people participating, and on the offerings to be sacrificed. And from these rituals the cleansing power of water has come into the Christian liturgical rites. We know that blessed, or holy, water came into the Church as early as the first half of the second century but the St. Matthew the Apostle is credited for being the first of the disciples of Christ to institute its usage in Christian ritual.

Ordinary Holy Water is used in the rite of the Asperges and by the faithful as they enter the church as they blessed themselves, marking themselves as baptized Christian believers. In early ages, one did not use the Holy Water for a blessing at the exit of the church; only as one entered, but this has changed due to variances in custom and practice. Ordinary Holy Water has a bit of salt added to it when first blessed although the formula may vary for doing so from diocese to diocese and parish to parish.

Baptismal Holy Water is traditionally blessed during the Lenten or Easter Season, typically on Pentecost or at the Vigil Mass on Holy Saturday. The Oil of the Catechumens and/or the Holy Chrism is added to it as part of the ritualistic blessing. This water is reserved for the sacrament of Baptism.

Gregorian Water is the blessed or holy water used for the consecration of new churches. It bears this name as Pope Gregory IX mandated it in 1238 for the sacred rites of blessing a new church structure. The Gregorian Water is used only for this purpose and has several other symbolic elements added to it at the time of blessing, namely altar wine, ashes from Ash Wednesday and salt.

Easter Water is that blessed water that is given out to the faithful after the Easter Vigil on Holy Saturday. In its earliest uses, this was the water that priests would bring to the homes of those seeking a blessing for their dwelling place

Note: After the reforms of the liturgy after Vatican Council II, an understanding of these historically and liturgically different waters was generally lost and simple blessed water suffices in many instances although the rubrics of Rome continue to mandate the various varieties of the Holy Water sacramental of the Church.

white feasts also known as 'white days' or as the *festa bianco;* the rare feast days in the Lenten Season, such as the Feast of Saint Joseph (March 19th), on which the somber, penitential severity of the season is temporarily abandoned for more festive spiritual celebrations. These days were inserted into the forty-day-long period of Lent so as to lift the spirits of the faithful after a prolonged period of penance and preparation. In Ireland and in nations where large numbers of Irish émigrés later settled, such as in the United States and Australia, the feast of Saint Patrick (March 17th) was also celebrated as a White Feast.

Whitsunday the Old English word for the feast of Pentecost.

wimple a white linen bib-like cloth that covered the throat, neck and ears of medieval women and some orders of nuns up to the close of Vatican Council II in 1965. It is also known as the conventual collar.

wine, altar the wine used in the Holy Sacrifice of the Mass must be genuine alcoholic wine made entirely from grapes, not grape juice, and without phosphates or other additives. In short, it must be wine in its purest form.

ALSO BY THIS AUTHOR

ALIX & MINNIE: Queen Alexandra of England & Empress Marie of Russia Book One: Royal Sisters Preparing for Greatness

ALIX & MINNIE: Queen Alexandra of England & Empress Marie of Russia Book Two: Adventure, Wealth and Scandal

ALIX & MINNIE: Queen Alexandra of England & Empress Marie of Russia Book Three: Widowhood, War, Revolution and Legacy

The Church Visible: The Ceremonial Life and Protocol of the Catholic Church – Revised Expanded Edition (Sterling Press, 2012)

The Church Visible: The Ceremonial Life and Protocol of the Catholic Church, Papal Commission, (Viking, 1996)

ABOUT THE AUTHOR

James-Charles Noonan is a noted author and historian with highly respected expertise in both royal and Vatican histories as well as in the disciplines of Vatican and international protocol. His particular areas of expertise cover Vatican history and ceremonial in the nineteenth and twentieth centuries as well as history of all the European royal houses, both reigning and non-regnant, during the same period.

Noonan is a Knight Grand Cross of the Holy Sepulchre of Jerusalem (the Holy See) and a Knight Commander of the Imperial House Order of Saint Michael the Archangel (the House of Romanov) amongst numerous other royal and international distinctions.

He resides in the United States in the hamlet of Gwynedd Valley.

Made in United States
North Haven, CT
30 December 2021

13872028R10115